DBT
Workbook for Adults

Simple & Effective Emotion Regulation & Mindfulness
Techniques Every Adult Needs - Guided DBT Skills

Caitlin McLean

Table of Contents

Introduction

OUT OF 300 MILLION Americans in the U.S., 40 million struggle with anxiety, making anxiety disorders the most common mental illness in the country (*Anxiety Disorders*, n.d.). For many, anxiety is just one symptom of a myriad of other health issues, like depression or other chronic illnesses. While many reasons are to blame for this mental health crisis, on a personal level, individuals can still achieve relief from their symptoms through various treatments. One of these methods is Dialectical Behavior Therapy (DBT).

DBT Workbook for Adults is a practical guide that provides easy-to-understand exercises for those wanting to increase communication, emotional regulation, and mindfulness.

Right now, you might be wondering:

- What is DBT?

- Where and when can I practice DBT?

- Why is this going to help me?

- How can I start DBT on my own?

That takes us to the objectives of the book. The goal of the readings are to:

- explain what DBT is in an easy and understandable way for beginners.

- provide simple and comprehensive exercises.

- assist those who need help managing their emotions.

- guide you toward better emotional regulation.

- show you how to deal with anxiety and stress.

- teach you how to handle your daily obstacles with practical methods.

Whether you are dealing with occasional anxiety or have been clinically diagnosed with a mental illness such as borderline personality disorder, you can find clarity in your thoughts in a simple, easy to understand way by implementing various DBT methods.

Getting Started

DBT is a type of treatment that can help those struggling with their emotions find a reduction of the negative impact their mental health has had on their life. The core focus of DBT is to notice, accept, and change thoughts that cause intense emotional turmoil.

Below are some frequently asked questions to help clear up any confusion and put your mind at ease before moving on to the exercises.

Does DBT Really Work?

DBT combines elements of Cognitive Behavioral Therapy (CBT) and mindfulness, both of which have been proven to be effective for the reduction of stress (American Psychological Association, 2017).

DBT aims to help users identify unhelpful thinking patterns and find a way to reduce these patterns for emotional clarity. Research shows it is effective for many types of patients struggling with personality disorders, parasuicidal patients, and those struggling with depression (Chapman, 2006). In addition, more recent studies show it to be an effective treatment method for patients struggling with obsessive-compulsive disorder (OCD) and other anxiety disorders (Pierce, 2021).

Since the aim is to reduce unhelpful and even harmful thoughts, anyone who struggles with a racing mind can find methods to help reduce limiting beliefs and increase emotional regulation.

Do I Need a Therapist to Practice DBT?

You might've heard about DBT in the past, or maybe a friend recommended this. If you have a therapist or are seeking treatment, continue on this avenue, as professional help can provide many needed benefits. However, if you don't have professional help, you will still be able to understand the theory and process of what will be covered in the readings.

This book was designed in a way to assist many individuals who are seeking clarity in their life. Those who are struggling emotionally will be able to achieve increased emotional regulation through practical exercises.

Doing the exercises with a professional can help you gain more insight, and others will hold you more accountable, however, it is not needed to see benefits.

How Long Will It Take To See Change?

Emotional change is fluid and can be hard to measure, but some might find slight relief after reading just a few exercises. You will notice greater changes after you finish the entirety of the book, so that will depend on your pace and reading plan.

The readings are organized into five parts, which also make the five chapters. The first will focus on theory and give you a simple understanding of DBT and the many benefits associated. Chapter 1 will dive into DBT in a more detailed way.

The next four chapters create the four corners of DBT: mindfulness, emotional regulation, distress tolerance, and interpersonal effectiveness. These will each have 15 exercises. You can follow along at your own pace with each activity. As there are 60 activities total, you can also allocate one exercise a day and track your progress over a two-month period. It can take time to see positive change, and patience is required for long-term results. Alternatively, you can read through it once or twice and return to the activities as needed.

How Do I Use This Book?

How this book is used will be based on your personal goals. Before getting started, take a moment to write down a few things you want to gain in regard to your emotional well-being. Are you struggling with panic attacks, anger outbursts, or mood swings? Identify the main issues and challenges you've been facing, as these can be the most pressing urgencies to address.

The readings will best be assisted by a journal to give you plenty of room to work with, though there will be space provided for the activities when needed. By using an outside notebook, word document, or digital journal, you give yourself the opportunity to go through the activities multiple times while tracking your progress.

Personal Assessment

Before getting started, and as you are creating goals for yourself, it can be useful to assess yourself to gain an understanding of where you are struggling the most. Below are 10 "yes or no" questions to help you understand how much anxiety, depression, or other mental illnesses are negatively impacting daily life. Keep track of your responses:

1. Do you struggle to control racing thoughts?

2. Do you notice your heart rate increasing or chest tightening when you feel anxious or stressed?

3. Have there been times when you wanted to isolate yourself from those around you?

4. Have you ever skipped a social event because your stress was too difficult to manage?

5. Do you experience waves of restlessness and fatigue?

6. Has stress ever brought on physical health symptoms like muscle aches, tension, or headaches?

7. Do your anxious thoughts make it difficult for you to focus and concentrate?

8. Have you experienced moments of, or urges to, self-harm?

9. Do you find yourself making impulsive decisions, often followed by waves of guilt or regret?

10. Are there times when you struggle to take care of yourself, such as skipping meals, failing to exercise, or neglecting hygiene habits?

If you answered yes to any of these, you will find help through DBT practices. If you found that you answered yes to a majority of them, you can use this as a time to reflect on some of the goals you have for positive change.

Going forward, remember to keep track of your progress. Writing things down increases the likelihood that you will remember them. Set your own pace. Unpacking deeply ingrained emotional habits can be challenging, and there will be times that it's required you to be accountable and push yourself even when it's uncomfortable. At the same time, find the balance between urgency and patience, as this is also a process that requires self-kindness.

Chapter 1

---︿---

What Is DBT?

EMOTIONS ARE POWERFUL. They are the energy source for our actions. What you do is triggered by what you think, and those thoughts are the way we translate our emotions. Emotions lead us to our greatest desires and assist us in achieving the things we need to survive.

Unfortunately, for many, emotions can be so powerful that they take the wheel of our life. Emotions, like rage and anger, can cause us to fight with other people or self-destruct in a way that only exacerbates our mental health.

Talk therapy, medical treatment, and professional help are not only expensive, but they can be daunting at first. While the help of a therapist is always recommended, you aren't doomed for misery if you don't have access to basic mental healthcare.

DBT is a type of therapy that was initially developed by Marsha Linehan. She sought to find a successful treatment that would assist suicidal women by helping them work through a multitude of problems by exploring and reworking thought processes (Chapman, 2006). The basis for the structure of DBT involves talk therapy, where the patient identifies and works through their emotions, motivations, and other driving factors that impact their mindset. The purpose is to help the individual regain basic autonomy over the things which pass through their mind.

Everyone feels emotions, but intensity differs among various people and situations. This form of psychotherapy doesn't just soothe your emotions temporarily; the focus is on how you can teach yourself to identify thoughts, feelings, and actions and make conscious and positive decisions for your overall health.

What Are Emotions?

You know what emotions feel like, but what are they, really? Emotions are reactions.

Whether you are reacting to a distressing situation or you're reacting to your own thoughts, emotions include the gut, instant, and first reaction to many types of stimuli.

Merriam-Webster defines emotions as "conscious mental reactions (such as anger or fear) subjectively experienced as strong feelings usually directed toward a specific object and typically accompanied by physiological and behavioral changes in the body." More simply put, Merriam-Webster also describes them as "a state of feeling."

Even defining emotions can be difficult because they are so subjective. You can feel the same emotion in two opposite situations, or alternatively, a recurring situation might make you feel opposite emotions each time.

There are four components of emotion (MacCann, 2021):

- situation

- focus

- meaning

- response

The situation you are in includes the surrounding factors or triggers of that emotion. This involves any people, triggering events, or even just symbols, colors, and shapes around you.

- Example: Seeing a picture of a kitten can make you feel happy, whereas witnessing a fight in public can cause distress.

Your focus includes whichever aspects of this situation gain the most of your attention. Even though certain events unfold in front of you, you can focus on different aspects.

- Example: Two people go to a restaurant with live music. One person focuses on the talent and passion of the musicians, feeling inspired. Another restaurant goer can't help but focus on the loud noises, causing them to feel overwhelmed and overstimulated.

The meaning behind the emotion depends on how you interpret the previous two parts. An emotion can mean something really intense is happening, and great change is needed. It could also indicate your opinions on a situation.

- Example: The annoyed restaurant patron from the previous example came with their two daughters. One daughter thinks it's funny that their dad is being somewhat of a curmudgeon, whereas the other is embarrassed by their father's behavior.

Lastly, your response is the outside, and sometimes internal, action that you take against these emotions. Even choosing to ignore your emotions is still a decision on how you are going to respond to the situation.

- Example: During a heated fight, a married couple begins calling each other names. They are both frustrated and hurt. One partner decides to walk away and cool down by responding to these emotions. The other decides to throw a glass against the wall in a fit of rage.

Emotions are often out of our control, but it is the meaning we ascribe and the response we choose that is within our control. Over time, you will be able to also refocus your attention on certain triggering aspects, making this emotional control easier. Identifying and reducing immediate responses is one aim of DBT.

Similar situations could bring out different emotions in two people, or a similar emotion can look different based on the situation. Consider emotions like:

- anger

- sadness

- happiness

- excitement

As you travel through the DBT exercises, the assistance of an emotion wheel might help. One you can use is Plutchik's Wheel of Emotions. This takes eight core emotions and breaks them down into more detailed words, helping you to begin the naming process. Many exercises within this book will aim to help you identify these emotions, but additional tools can help.

Emotional dysregulation can lead to anxiety when left ignored (Amstadter, 2008). If the process were a simple one, however, more people would be living happier lives, and fewer would suffer from debilitating feelings.

That takes us to the four corners of DBT. Together, these make up the levels of behavior therapy you will travel through in the readings. Making long-lasting change requires that you break down tasks into smaller, more manageable parts. As you travel through the four corners, you will start to see the basic guide for how emotional management will be possible.

Four Corners of DBT

Initially for helping those with borderline personality disorder (BPD), DBT is now effective for anyone who needs more emotional regulation in their life. The framework for DBT is made up of four parts:

- mindfulness

- emotional regulation

- distress tolerance

- interpersonal effectiveness

When one is able to be mindful, work through crises, increase personal skills, and prevent emotions from overpowering us in the future, it can be very effective in helping to manage mental health.

Mindfulness involves breaking down awareness of your situation and pausing the flow of thoughts that might be disrupting the required actions around you. For example, noticing that you are feeling anxious because you're hungry can lead you to eat a snack so you are better focused when you return to work.

Emotional regulation is necessary after we become mindful because then it's required that the emotion is either acknowledged, addressed, or remedied. Knowing you're mad is good, but now, how will you regulate those feelings to ensure you don't lash out and cause more issues?

Distress tolerance then follows. Even when there is an emphasis placed on mindfulness and regulation, there will be outside triggers and other stressful events which can lead to additional anxiety. What if you are angry, and someone keeps pushing you for a reaction? Knowing how to stop emotional reactions at the exact moment they happen and before they become overly heightened gives you the opportunity to prevent destructive behavior from following.

Lastly, interpersonal effectiveness encapsulates your strength and skills pertaining to how you interact with those around you. Becoming aware of your own feelings is an important aspect of reducing mental health, but we also need to know how to function in the world around us and work with other people to prevent and address conflict.

There are four remaining chapters, each one exploring the different branches of these subjects. They are separated so you can easily navigate the readings as you travel through these four corners. Before beginning, identify which of the four you might be struggling with the most. After completing the exercises, reassess to see where you gained the most insight and where you might want to continue to focus going forward.

The Benefits of DBT

Someone choosing DBT might want to consider the benefits to know whether or not this is the right decision.

DBT is beneficial for those who are seeking non-medication (*Dialectical Behavior Therapy*, n.d.). Having to try various kinds of prescriptions to find something that's right isn't an easy process. The fluctuation of emotions and uncertainty is hard to process, and advocating for yourself adds a new layer of confusion when you're already seeking help.

DBT also provides the ability to self-manage and build long-lasting skills. Some therapies or medications are temporary or used only as needed. DBT builds skills within you to provide effectiveness permanently.

DBT can help reduce (*Dialectical Behavior Therapy*, n.d.):

- impulsive behavior

- self-destructive decisions

- suicidal thoughts

- disordered eating

DBT can also:

- improve relationships

- help predict and manage triggers

- reduce anxiety

The key in DBT will be your own initiative. If you are not working with a therapist, it is up to you to stay diligent and hold yourself accountable to see real change. The more you repeat the exercise, the more likely you will be to see an improvement overall, allowing you to gain the previously mentioned benefits.

How to Use This Book

There are a few more important things to cover to ensure you make the most of the book.

First, start with a main goal. Do you want to reduce negative thought processes? Do you wish to mediate your anxiety disorder? Are you looking for a way to increase your mind's ability for natural regulation? Keep a singular goal in mind, and from there, break it down into further wishes or objectives as you travel through the readings.

Having a point to change from is a great place to start and provides you with an aspect of comparison once you make it to the end of the book. In addition, having a goal means that you have hope for your future. This is a great point of motivation to keep you focused when future exercises might present a challenge.

Going through the exercises chronologically can help, but you are free to jump around as needed and should return to the reading exercises even after you've finished the book. This won't affect whether or not you are able to gain insight from the exercises, though, keep in mind they were chosen in this specific structure to help ease you through the activities/lessons.

DBT is best used daily. Whether you spend 10 minutes or five hours on an exercise is up to you; what matters most is consistency and commitment to elicit real change.

If you know someone with similar goals or who has been thinking about trying DBT, you might also find that a partner can help you get more from the exercises. They can hold you accountable, and you can share some of the things you learned the most from, also getting help for any areas you might still find confusing or difficult. Some activities can be deeply personal and triggering, however, so this is still something you can keep personal.

When actually following the exercises, do your best to remove distractions around you. Turn off music, background TV, and even your phone. Notifications and background noises will pull your focus, taking away some of your ability to give your all to the exercise. You can certainly still passively read for additional understanding, but remember that giving 100% of your focus to these activities will ensure you stay on track.

Remember to keep a journal to help you expand as needed and find a pace that works uniquely for you. There's no wrong way to use DBT, but following these best practices will help ensure effectiveness.

Overview: Introduction

DBT is a type of talk and reflective therapy involving one's ability to notice thought and behavior patterns and manage them through emotions and actions. This isn't an instant method or a cure-all for mental illnesses. However, DBT will enable users to know how to recognize unwanted and intense emotions with realistic and practical methods to reduce the side effects that have been brought on.

Every human has emotions. They serve us a very important purpose. Unfortunately, they can also be challenging to manage. With dedication and commitment, even the most challenging emotions can turn into something valuable.

Chapter 2

Mindfulness

THE FIRST CORNER OF DBT is mindfulness, as this is the foundation for which you start to build the other four skills. Marsha Linehan, the DBT founder, explains mindfulness using three states of mind (Bray, 2013):

- logical

- emotional

- wise

Your logical mind is the objective and factual information you assess in the situation. Emotional states of mind are the inner feelings we have, and the wise mind is how we respond to these states.

Mindfulness is focused on observation. By building awareness around these states of mind, you can effectively reduce unwanted emotions and learn how to sit with challenging feelings. What things are happening around you in the present moment, and how are they affecting, affected by, or related to your emotions? Answering this question is the important first step.

Awareness increases when you notice your senses and the way that your body feels in conjunction with your mind. Are you feeling sick or light-headed because you are overwhelmed? Do you have a stomach ache because you need to drink some water? It's easy to let the physical effects of anxiety contribute to the intensity of the feelings we're already struggling with, so bodily awareness helps keep this type of panic at bay.

After making these observations, we must know how to avoid judgment on these emotions. Rather than blaming yourself, or another person, for your emotions, you can recognize that you are simply experiencing feelings, a normal human occurrence. As you sit with these emotions without judgment, the side effects will start to fade, allowing you a clearer head to make productive decisions.

Neutrality allows you to find mindfulness in a place of neither good nor bad, positive or negative. How you feel determines how you act, so feeling neutral gives you the best chance to make objective, logical decisions.

The last part of mindfulness is maintaining the focus that you built and participating in the tasks around you. Completing a task passively is one thing, but doing them with concentration while quieting the mind is a different level of mindfulness. Anxious thoughts can still sit in the back of your mind, even if you're actively doing something physical.

The best time for mindfulness activities is during your daily routine or while trying to focus. Emotional awareness should be used all the time—not just when you're feeling stressed or panicked. This helps create a more natural, heightened awareness, enabling better management in the future.

Observation

The first part of mindfulness is observing your surroundings to bring about a sense of awareness. What objects, people, noises, and other physical things surround you? What are the thoughts in your mind? When these are disjointed, it distracts from the moment. Focusing on what your friend is saying is hard when you're ruminating about the stressful thing that happened at work today.

Examples of scenarios when you might use observation skills:

- You're trying to study but can't focus on what you're reading.

- You're waiting for your plane to take off and starting to feel nervous.

- When you're out at a restaurant with a friend, you start to get anxious as you're talking, and second-guessing what you're saying.

- It's the night before a big job interview and you can't sleep.

- It's 7:00 p.m., you're bored and feeling blue, and you can't decide if you should go to bed early or watch a movie.

Situations vary, but these are some examples of when it would be good to implement observation exercises.

Exercise: Single Object

Mindfulness is an exercise that you can have regardless of the situation, but having a specific object to focus on in the first place is a good place to start. Wherever you are in the room right now, grab an object that you can hold in your hands. It should be something that is light enough to pick up with one hand and small enough that you can see most of the object from all angles.

First, set this object down in front of you on the table. Notice how the object is connecting to the surface that you placed it on. What angles are touching? What does the shape look like on the table? What support does the object need to be in this specific spot? Are there any shadows? Are there any holes that you can see through?

Pick up the object and look at it while it is in your hand. Is it easy to move around? How does it move between your fingers? What does that object feel like? What are the materials that it is made of? Can you squeeze this object? Can you bend or shape it in a different way? Would you describe it as being flat or round? Is it big for what it is? Or is it small for what it is? Of course, it's small enough that you can hold it in your hand, but maybe it's something that's bigger than the average size. For example, perhaps you're holding an extra-large, juicy apple. Maybe you have a big quarter compared to other smaller coins like a penny. What are the details of this object? What are the ridges? Is there anything printed on this? What letters, colors, and other shapes do you see? What other forms or images are spread across the surface of this object?

Now, hold the object in your hand and close your eyes. Ensure that there is nothing on the object that you could hurt yourself with. If so, then choose a different object for this part of the activity. With your eyes closed, run your fingers along the edge of the object. Visualize what it looks like in your mind. Use the images that you just saw to try and recreate this object with your imagination. Do your best to see the detailed color of this original object. Move it around and notice any sensation that you have as you use this object in your hand.

After you're done moving this object around, take a moment to reflect on what sensations you felt while this was happening. Were you able to distract your mindset from the things that have been pulling your focus? This is a good exercise to use whenever you're feeling anxious and need to calm down in the moment.

Exercise: Body Scan

This next activity is known as a body scan. This is one of the most common methods of mindfulness because it helps us focus on every part of our body.

Notice the way that the air is traveling through your body as you focus on relaxing and letting go of tension. Read through this visualization, and then imagine it after with your eyes closed.

- Imagine that you're standing on a platform.

- The platform slowly lowers you into a pool of water.

- The water is warm and feels good; this is not a scary or stressful situation.

- Let any muscle tension fizzle away.

- Relax your shoulders, arms, abdomen, hips, and legs.

- Picture yourself with your feet flat, standing on this platform.

- It slowly starts to move down.

- The water rises up over at the bottom of your feet.

- You're moving extremely slowly. You are safe at this moment, and there is no present danger.

- Simply notice the way that the water starts to rise above your feet.

- The water closes in over the top of your foot, and now you're ankle-deep.

- It continues to rise up through your shin and the back of your calf.

- The water is now touching your kneecap and rising toward your thigh.

- You can feel the water in your groin area and on the back of your legs.

- The water rises up around your hips, and you can feel it pass over your belly button.

- The water is now at your armpits, and your hands are fully submerged. It is like a warm blanket, and you feel safe.

- You can feel the water travel up your arms until it closes over your shoulder.

- It stops at your neck.

- Take a moment and lean your head back, picturing yourself submerging the top of your head in the water.

- Keep visualizing yourself in this tank.

- Now, the water is lowering as the platform rises again.

- The water is scanning back down your body.

- The water is moving down over your chest area and back to your hips.

- The surface of the water is now around the top of your legs.

- As you continue to slowly rise, the water passes over your knees, your shins, your ankles, and your feet.

- Open your eyes and take a breath.

- Notice the way that you're holding your body now.

Whenever you are feeling your muscles tense and your anatomy getting stressed out, you can go back through this body scan exercise. Picture the water rising over the entirety of your body, feeling these calming effects. What you will notice is that some of the tension that normally adds to your anxiety actually starts to fade away.

Exercise: Mindful Eating

Mindfulness is an activity that we sometimes participate in without even realizing it. When was the last time you were really focused on your work? Or maybe you got lost in schoolwork, like a research project. Can you recall a movie that you got lost in? Did you ever read a book only to finish and forget that you had been in a fictional world?

Sometimes our mind becomes enthralled when we give 100% of our focus to specific activities. One common activity that we all participate in is eating. Multiple times a day, you have to eat in order to nourish your body. Often, we start to think of this as more of a passive activity. You'll see people walking down the street with food in hand as they rush to work. You'll notice drivers trying to hold a sandwich while they navigate their commute. At night, we order our food and plop down on the couch in front of the TV with our tasty meal.

While simultaneously eating during other activities isn't always a bad thing, we still have to learn how to be mindful when we are nourishing our body.

Mindful eating is a habit that can help you maintain your eating habits without over or under eating because of outside distractions. For this exercise, grab your favorite fruit or vegetable. Choose a specific whole food, meaning it only has a singular ingredient, like an apple or an orange.

Turn off any music and all other distractions around you. Find a comfortable place to sit.

Set this fruit in front of you. Take a moment to go back through the singular object exercise and identify some elements of this object. What shape does it have? What texture is there? Where did this come from? Describe the colors and any smell or other senses that are activated simply by this fruit or vegetable sitting in front of you.

For the sake of this exercise, let's envision eating an orange.

First, you're going to reach out in front of you and hold the orange. Keep it in your hand for a moment, and let the textures pass through your fingers. You can feel the rough rind. Perhaps there's a waxy coat from the grocery store that you purchased it from. Maybe it is still a little damp after having rinsed it off.

Now, start to peel the orange. You can use a utensil if you prefer, or you can peel it back with just your hand. Peel off the layer slowly. Ensure that you are in a quiet area so you can listen to the sounds as the fruit becomes peeled. Notice all of the sensations that you're experiencing as you go through this process.

Once the fruit is peeled, simply pull off a slice of the orange. Take a small bite and hold it in your mouth for a moment before you begin chewing. Don't suck on the fruit. At first, simply let it sit on your tongue and notice what happens in your brain and in your body. Pay attention to your urges right now. You likely have the urge to chew or swallow.

Wait a few moments and sit with mindfulness around this object.

Allow yourself to start chewing and tasting the fruit.

Notice all the sensations across your tongue as you chew. Slowly swallow and take another bite. As you continue eating, notice the different parts of your body that are activated during this process.

Take in every flavor that this food provides. What other images pop into your head as you're eating this specific food? Perhaps you are thinking about eating oranges on a bright sunny day. Perhaps you recall a time when you were sticky from leftover orange juice. Maybe orange reminds you of a specific person, or the color triggers a descriptive scenario. As you continue eating and being mindful in this moment, notice any emotions that pass through your mind.

Try practicing mindful eating at least once a week, if you can set aside one meal a day, even better.

The more that you practice mindful eating, the more you will not only appreciate the food that you're eating, but you'll also create awareness around some emotions that you have attached to this very normal and human habit.

Sensation

Noticing sensations helps you to better describe the things you're feeling. Paying attention to what your mind, body, and heart is doing will distract you and pull your focus back to the present moment. Connecting to your body helps you notice signs of anxiety before they can manifest into more intense emotions. For example, if you notice your breathing starts to increase and your leg is tapping, you can steady your breathing and focus on calming down rather than letting anxiety build.

Examples of scenarios when you might use sensation skills:

- You want to add a relaxation technique to your daily routine.

- You're struggling to catch your breath and feeling like your chest is tightening.

- You feel the urge to cry but aren't sure why.

- You're stuck ruminating on a past mistake or regret.

- You're feeling anxious before going to a social gathering.

The more you practice noticing your senses, the more frequently you will enable yourself to ascribe understanding to the thoughts passing through your mind, enhancing situational mindfulness.

Exercise: Meditation

Mindfulness is an exercise that anybody can practice at any time of the day. Meditation is an exercise that takes things a step further.

Rather than mindfully living and bringing more awareness to everyday situations, meditation requires that you pick a specific time to actually meditate.

Sometimes people think of meditation as a Zen state of mind, void of thoughts. That's not always the case.

Meditation is the acceptance of our thoughts. It's learning how to sit with them passively in your mind without holding judgment or making assumptions based on these ideas and visions.

To practice meditating, find a specific area in your home to meditate. It's important to have a separate space that you can dedicate to this exercise so that your mind doesn't get triggered into other areas. For example, if you try to meditate in your bed, where you sleep every night, you might get tired and want to take a nap. If you decide to take a nap after you meditate, that is fine, but start in a different area first. You might also try to meditate on the couch where you sit and watch TV or play video games. Wherever you choose to sit has muscle memories associated with it that can make it harder for your brain to snap into a meditative state.

Once you find a specific location, remove all distractions. Just like for the previous exercises, turn off all music or TV shows and put your phone in a different room to ensure that it doesn't add any more distractions.

Even pets might be distracting, so if you can, find an area where you can close the door and be completely alone. Sit in a comfortable position where you don't have any tension placed on specific parts of your body. Laying down is fine for meditating, but you can also sit cross-legged or in a comfortable chair.

To begin meditating, first become aware of your breathing patterns.

Take a big deep breath that you feel passes all the way into the depths of your stomach. Let that breath out completely. Don't cut it off before you take another breath in. Let all of that air travel out and really clean out your lungs. Continue this deep breathing until you find a regular pace that's comfortable for you. Keep your arms and legs relaxed, and every time you notice them tense back up, take another deep belly breath.

Right now, at the beginning stages of meditation, you might find that your mind is running rapidly with thoughts. You can try counting down in order to help you disperse some of these thoughts, at least momentarily. Start at 10 and count down. If you are still struggling with your thoughts, you can count back up and keep this pattern up until your thoughts become regulated.

Then try to focus on simply nothing. Thoughts are going to pass into your mind but push them away gently. You don't have to yell at yourself to stop having a thought. You don't have to panic because anxious thoughts have made their way into your mindset.

Pretend that you are in water and a leaf is floating toward you on the surface. Use your hand to gently push that leaf away. You wouldn't grab that leaf and go to the trouble of getting out of the pool to throw it away. You wouldn't grab that leaf, hold it, and crumple it up in your hands. You would simply push that leaf away and ignore it. It might float back around you but simply push it away once again.

Continue bringing your focus back to your breathing, your body, and how you're holding the entirety of your anatomy.

Set a timer to ensure that you meditate for at least five minutes. The more you practice, the easier it will be to get into this meditative state and to work through some of your thoughts.

Meditation is a great way to reset your mind for the day, and it can also act as a great transition between different parts of your life. For example, getting home from work might bring a lot of stress into your household. Instead of going right into your household duties, you might take 10 minutes to meditate to help get your brain into a new state of mind.

Eventually, work your way up to meditating for 30 minutes or even an hour. You can meditate when you wake up in the morning or before you go to bed at night to help maximize your body's energy restoration periods.

Exercise: Practice Observing

Observation in the moment can happen wherever you are. You already have the skills in your body. Now it's time to unlock them to use their fullest potential.

Our observation skills are based on our five senses. There are some individuals who might not have all five abilities, but even when one is impaired, the others can be effectively used for observation. These are your five senses:

- sight

- hearing

- touch

- taste

- smell

Start by noticing what each of these senses feels like based on the situation around you. Below are two different charts to help inspire methods of evaluating your senses:

Description of each:

Sight	This is based on what visuals are in front of you. Pay attention to objects, angles, and the way spaces are separated through doors and archways. How tall are the ceilings, and what colors make up the sights you take in? Where does your attention go? What does this image say about the space?
Hearing	The things you hear include voices from others, or perhaps what noises their actions make. This is also inclusive of background noises, humming, buzzing, or natural noises. Notice multiple layers of noises, tones, and volume levels. Identifying the source of the noise provides more sensory aspects to identify.
Touch	Touch is based on what physical things you feel with your body. This includes your hands. What things are in reach? Touch is also based on the other parts of our bodies we can feel, like our clothes, the things we're sitting on, or what is beneath our feet. Grabbing something small to hold and touch can help you focus this sense more easily.
Taste	While there are many situations that we are in that don't involve specifically tasting something, we can still draw attention to this sense. What is something around you that you could taste, if needed? Perhaps there is a

	mint or other object around that you could try tasting. This could also lead you to snap into the moment by grabbing a drink or sip of water.
Smell	Lastly, identifying the things you smell can pull your focus to the surrounding situation. What scents are taking up your attention? Like taste, there might not be an aspect that is easy to identify in relation to your sense of smell, but you can envision the scent of items around you, like a flower or the scent of the tree outside your window.

Example 1: Picture a common situation—standing in line for security at the airport. You're cutting it close to boarding, and the line seems to be taking an especially long time to get through. You're feeling panicked and overwhelmed, so you use your five senses to keep you present in the moment.

Sight	You see the floor. It is light blue with dark blue specks. You see the people in front of you and start to look at each of their shoes. You don't make judgments, you simply identify these things as you travel through the sights.
Hearing	You hear the chatter of the others in line. You listen for any music or other background sounds. You can hear the tweet of a bird that happened to fly in.
Touch	You can feel your bag in your hand. With your other, you pay attention to how your hand is in a fist, and you release this tension.

Taste	You taste the mint you had in your bag. You keep some on you to help give you something to focus on. You think about the water you are going to taste after you make it through security.
Smell	Lastly, you can smell the coffee coming from the cafe across from security. You envision yourself grabbing a cup.

Before you know it, you made it through security with ease, helping to slow down panicked thoughts. Though you might still be feeling anxious before the flight, you've at least reduced some of the panicked thoughts that had initially started to pile up.

Use this empty chart below to fill in your own situation. Call back to a time when you were especially overwhelmed with ruminating thoughts, or overstimulated by a stressful environment. Try to recall these five senses or think of things you could identify if in a future stressful situation.

Sight	
Hearing	

Touch	
Taste	
Smell	

Exercise: Nose-Mouth Breathing

A body with unwanted emotions might start struggling from some of the negative side effects that are brought on by these feelings. This might include things such as a rapid heart rate, muscle tension, body aches, teeth grinding, chest tightening, and uneven breathing.

There is one exercise that can help instantly alleviate some of these negative side effects of unwanted emotions. This is referred to as nose-mouth breathing. The focus of this exercise will be on regulating the breath that travels in and out of your body in order to keep you focused in the moment and prevent spiraling thoughts.

By focusing on your breathing, you will relax your shoulders, arms, and other muscles to help ensure that you can find a state of peace.

Start by recognizing the pattern with which you are breathing in this moment. Are you short of breath? Do you feel like your chest is tight? Do you feel like you are dizzy or lightheaded?

1. Notice how the air is traveling in and out of your body.

2. Breathe in a more regulated pattern.

3. Only breathe in through your nose and only exhale through your mouth.

4. Breathe in.

5. Breathe out.

To take this a step further, you can add in a mindful object, or you can use a focal point in the room around you.

1. Find something in the room with an even number of sides. This might be the shape of a window, or perhaps your phone in your hand.

2. Use your eyes or finger to trace each side as you breathe in and out.

3. Breathe in through your nose as you trace one side.

4. Breathe out through your mouth as you trace the neck side.

5. Repeat this process again.

Continue following the pattern of this shape to help alleviate rising reactions.

Try counting up to five and down from five as you breathe in and out. This will help ensure that you are breathing at a slow and steady pace.

Another activity to add with nose-mouth breathing is to trace a circle in your hand. Breathe in as you trace clockwise, and breathe out as you trace counterclockwise. This forces you to pull all of your senses into the palm of your hand so that you have more control and regulation over your breathing in the moment.

Whenever you are feeling overwhelmed with panic or paralyzed with anxiety, you can focus on nose-mouth breathing to pull you into the mindful present.

Judgment

A core part of developing DBT skills is knowing how to sit with your emotions without judgment. These activities aim to help you take the awareness and sensations you recognize and analyze them without being overly self-critical.

Releasing judgment ensures you're not left making assumptions based on physical feelings you're experiencing.

Examples of scenarios when you might use judgment skills:

- You have judgmental thoughts about another person.

- You're ruminating on regretful situations and casting blame on yourself.

- You're struggling with self-deprecation before an important event.

- Someone makes a comment about your appearance, and you can't help but let it bug you the rest of the day.

- Shame and embarrassment feelings keep causing distraction.

Judgment is a hard mental habit to break because we need judgment to survive. You judge whether or not food is too hot to bite. You judge if it's warm enough outside to leave your jacket at home. You judge which apartment suits your needs when finding a new home. Excessive judgment, however, can be cast internally, perpetuating unwanted emotions through our dialectical behavior.

Exercise: Wise Mind

The wise mind is the cohesion of your reasonable and your emotional mind (Lineham, 2015). On one hand, you have a reasoning and logic system that your brain uses to make judgments around you. On the other hand, you can be driven by emotions, passions, and the things that really get under your skin.

Logically, you know that it's not beneficial to be mean to other people. Despite this logic, sometimes, when you're feeling a state of heightened emotions, you act based on your emotional mind.

- Example: when running late to work, you act emotionally and decide to speed, even though logically, you know you're putting yourself at risk of getting a speeding ticket.

Connecting the logical and emotional mind will provide more cohesive thoughts based on both reason and inner feelings. This control will not only drive you to take the best steps systematically, but you will also have the focus to place toward understanding and reducing complex emotions.

Both minds provide value; each side of your brain is something that is needed in order for your survival. Connecting both sides helps to center yourself. There are a few different activities that you can use to help connect these two sides together. Each part of your brain is responsible for a different part of your body, and working with the mind and body at the same time will help you connect these two important driving factors together. Follow these activities below to help you connect both sides of your brain:

1. Start switching up what side you use when brushing your teeth at night and in the morning. Most of us have a dominant hand—either right or left. When you go to grab your toothbrush and toothpaste every single morning, you likely use the same hands. Use a Post-it note to remind yourself to practice this mindful activity in the morning. Brushing your teeth with the opposite hand makes your mind connect to itself.

2. Another activity to try is one similar to the deep breathing exercise that we mentioned previously. This time, instead of breathing out through your mouth, breathe in and breathe out alternating, between nostrils. To do this, press on your left nostril and breathe in through your right. Hold your breath for a moment as you switch sides, and press out on your right nostril as you breathe out through the left. Continue this pattern and switch up which side you are inhaling and exhaling through to help reconnect and center your mindset.

3. For the next activity, reach in front of you and touch all 10 of your fingertips together. Gently press your hands together, slowly stretching your fingers until your palms are touching. Now with your hands flat in front of you, lift your arms and point your fingers toward the sky. Hold this in the air for a moment as you breathe in. Now as you exhale, lower your elbows keeping your hands together. Have your hands go behind your head to help stretch your shoulders out. As you continue exhaling, breathe in and out as you alternate, slowly raising and lowering your arms.

4. Next time you are sitting on the couch or working at your office desk, notice when you get up and move to a new location. Try to walk backward as you travel from one destination to the next. This forces you to focus on what you are doing more and increases the level at which you pay attention to your surroundings.

5. Next time you have to write something down, try using your opposite hand. Just like as previously mentioned with the toothpaste activity, it can be difficult to do this at first, but when you really concentrate, you help to connect your mind.

After participating in some of these wise mind activities, pay attention to how you feel with your emotions. What paths does your mind follow? Find the connections between your brain to help keep you centered between your logical and emotional brain.

Exercise: Making Judgements

Making judgments can lead us to create specific boxes for how we evaluate life. This can limit our perspective, leading to black-and-white thinking. For example, being late to walk can lead you to judge the day as being "bad," therefore expecting more bad things to happen throughout the remainder of the day. This causes you to hyperfixate on those "bad" aspects, losing sight of the other good things that occurred throughout the day.

In another example, judging how someone dresses creates preconceived notions for their behavior, limiting your perspective on who they are as a person.

Remember, making judgments isn't always a bad thing, but it's important to be conscious of the judgments we make since they can heavily influence our actions.

Begin tracking your judgments to notice what underlying patterns might have been driving your behavior. There are a few important aspects to focus on:

- **Judgment:** Identify the initial judgment for what it is.

- **Trigger:** What situation, person, or occurrence triggered this judgment? Did it pop into your head randomly, or was there another reason for this judgment?

- **Time:** Knowing the time could impact this judgment as well. For example, maybe you were tired, overwhelmed, or hungry, therefore in a more agitated world.

- **Reaction:** What is your reaction to this judgment? Did you feel guilty for having it, or did you act on the feelings it brought on?

Below is an example of what tracking these emotions might look like:

Date: October 20, 2023

Judgment	Trigger	Time	Reaction
The world is a terrible place.	I didn't get the job I wanted.	2:00 p.m.	I couldn't focus on work the rest of the day, feeling hopeless.
My partner is really messy and disrespects me.	They didn't do the dishes after dinner.	6:00 p.m.	I ignored them throughout the rest of the night.
I'm really unattractive and need to change ASAP.	I have a party tonight and need to get ready quickly.	7:00 p.m.	I decided to cancel my plans at the last minute and stayed home instead.

Keep track of your judgments using the empty chart below. A judgment against others can create a standard for how you judge yourself. Identifying these judgments can help you reduce how many judgments you give to yourself, others, and situations over time.

Date:

_____

Judgment	Trigger	Time	Influence	Reaction

Neutrality

Mindfulness means seeing your thoughts and emotions as neither good nor bad and, instead, embracing them with neutrality.

Examples of scenarios when you might use neutrality skills:

- Assuming you're going to get in trouble at work after you get a call from your boss.

- When you're stuck in a cycle of believing there is no hope in the future based on emotions you're feeling in the present.

- Your partner starts to argue about how you're splitting the chores.

- A coworker sent a frustrating email that started to make your blood boil.

Once a challenging emotion is sensed, the next important step is to approach it with a focus on neutrality. You can't stop conflict, but you can be patient and find a sense of security as it passes.

Exercise: Beach of Thoughts

One way to help you make better sense of your emotions is to put them into a visual scenario. Think of a place that is calming and relaxing to you. Notice things that pass through this specific space. What are these passing objects? People? Animals? Clouds?

They come and go in a constant and unpredictable path. Every time you have a feeling, you don't have to grab onto this and hold on to those emotions. You can simply let them pass through, just as we let time pass through the space that we are in.

Your emotions are reflections of the things that you experience in the moment. Let them pass by rather than clinging onto them. When you hang on to feelings of the past, you never let yourself move forward into the present, therefore, taking more and more time away from the future.

For this exercise, visualize a beach. A beach has been chosen as the example space because this is a common relaxing location for many people. Close your eyes and focus on deep breathing, or alternate breathing through different nostrils, as you regulate the oxygen entering and exiting your body. Follow these steps as you visualize the beach:

1. Picture yourself sitting on the coarse sand. You place your hands around you and feel all of the grains that create the comfortable position that you're in. Pick up a handful of sand. In this handful are thousands of little, tiny rocks and other pieces of earth that create the sand. Envision yourself slowly turning your hands so that the sand pours out. This is how you can visualize your thoughts. You have so many thoughts a day. You can pick up a handful of thoughts and scoop them up. You can hold on to these thoughts, you can put them in a bottle, and you can keep them forever. However, you can also simply pick them up and let them go.

2. Now, visualize yourself walking toward the water. You step into the water and feel the waves wash over your legs. Some waves are big, and some waves are small. No matter what the waves continue to do, they don't pause. They don't stop, and they don't linger. They wash over you and pass away. Use this to also help you remember how your thoughts rise and fall throughout the day. Some thoughts and emotions feel like big strong waves that might knock you down. Others look big and come in slowly as they settle around your legs. Your thoughts are different shapes and sizes. Sometimes they seem scarier than they are, and sometimes they might hit you out of nowhere. Always remember that eventually, just like the wave, they will wash away.

3. Finally, look up at the sky and see how the clouds pass over you. Some are large and block the sun from hitting you. Others dissipate as they travel across the sky. Your thoughts are just like the clouds. They keep passing over you. They change shapes as they move in different directions. You can look at a cloud and see a shape. Other clouds will be confusing formations. Some days will be cloudier than others, and sometimes

clouds will bring on rain. Sometimes clouds will block the light. No matter what the sky looks like now, it will change.

Use these analogies of the beach to help you remember your emotions. When you are feeling like the day is cloudy and the ocean is thrashing, remember to keep breathing until these things subside.

A beach might not be your chosen relaxation spot; that is fine. Think of a safe space where you feel like everything is going to be okay. This should make you feel neutral, peaceful, and secure. Consider what passes through this space and how it changes over time. The visual representation in your mind can allow emotional coping when your thoughts are running.

Exercise: Objective Thinking

Objective thinking is an activity that can help keep you focused and mindful of the present moment. Objective thinking can be used as a way to assist in your ability to check the facts. You can follow the **FACT** acronym. This involves:

- framing

- attempt at meaning

- comparisons

- tone

When you are thinking subjectively, that means you are not following the facts, and instead, are focused on opinion. Follow the four parts of this acronym when assessing the facts:

1. Framing refers to the structures that create your view of a specific image. Go to your phone or a photo album and pick out a picture. In your hands, you see the whole picture. Now, place your hand over half the picture. Whether you cover up the top half, the left half, or you cover up a diagonal portion of the image, simply focus on the half of the

picture that is uncovered and think of a few ways to describe what you see. Now, cover up the opposite half and do the same thing.

2. What do you notice about the different aspects of the picture? For example, let's say that there's a picture of somebody smiling in a room. You cover up the bottom half, so you only see the person's torso and their smiling face. You can see somebody who's really happy. When you cover up the top half, what you see on the bottom half is a messy room filled with clutter and trash. This may indicate that this person is disorganized or dissatisfied with their surroundings.

3. In the whole picture, you see somebody who is able to live in this space and be happy. When you frame a situation, you only look at certain aspects. Objective thinking means looking at the whole picture and removing the frames. Now, take that picture and visualize what other aspects surround that image that aren't even seen in the photograph. This can help you open up new perspectives so that when you are looking at a situation, you're not stuck just by what is seen in the frame.

4. The next part of objective thinking involves finding an attempt at meaning. Notice the way that you are looking at the situation and trying to find meaning from what is there, as this can cloud judgment. In the example with the whole picture, you might be creating meaning based on previous facts that you know, or assumptions about the things that you see within that picture. When looking at the whole picture, you are removing any attempts at finding meaning, and instead, you are focused on identifying all the aspects that create the objective standpoint. This can help you remove some of your biases so that you can see the situation more neutrally.

5. Next, think about comparisons. We often make assumptions and create subjective opinions based on previous information that we have. We compare it side by side with other situations, and we juxtapose it in our mindset based on what we want to come out of the situation. When trying to think objectively, identify the way that you are making comparisons to help give you a fair stance.

6. Lastly, think about the tone. How you view an image is going to change based on the tone that you have at the time. If you are in a good mood, you might walk through a situation focusing on the things that make you happy. If you are in a bad mood, you might walk through the situation, highlighting and emphasizing the things that help validate your emotion. What tone are you in? What voice are you using to describe the situation? Keep your tone objective, and you'll find that it's easier to form objective standpoints.

Participation

Taking action is also a part of mindfulness. When you are mindful, it's important to focus on one thing at a time and give it your full attention. This helps improve focus on what you're doing, making it even easier to distract yourself from difficult thoughts.

Examples of scenarios when you might use participation skills:

- You're writing an important paper for school.

- You're deep cleaning and reorganizing your closet.

- You're making homemade bread from scratch.

- You and your partner are enjoying a peaceful silence as the sunsets.

- You're starting a new workout routine.

No matter what you are doing at the moment, give it your full attention. You will learn how to be more present each day when you make a dedication to absorbing the moment for what it is. Reduce the urge to multitask, as this requires more energy as your brain switches back and forth. The average attention span has been decreasing over the years, and it's important we relearn how to enthusiastically focus on the important things in front of us.

Exercise: Mindful Tasks

Another mindful exercise is to use mindful tasks. This involves:

- T: total focus

- A: acceptance

- S: strategy

- K: knowledge

To complete something mindfully means to give it total focus. This requires eliminating distractions and reducing attention given to things that are pulling your focus. Total focus means turning off music when it comes time to eat. It means shutting off the background movie when you have to study. Mindful living means giving the entirety of your attention and senses to the specific chosen task.

The next letter in the TASK acronym is acceptance. This means completing this task without any judgment. It means letting go of preconceived notions, standards, or the urge to be a perfectionist when trying to finish this task.

Focus on strategy. What strategy are you using to complete this task? Often, this is based on the outcome, so you have to pick a strategy that is going to give you the results that you desire. You have to come up with a step-by-step process to get through this task, and that will help give you even more focus so that you're not thinking about what you have to do next.

The last letter of the acronym to remember is knowledge. Knowledge is what you use based on past experiences to help you complete this task. It also involves taking knowledge from the situation and adding that to your expertise. Next time you complete this task, you can be much more mindful when doing it; therefore, you get more out of the experience. Knowledge is something that we can always grow, so remember to bring awareness to help really compound the effectiveness of your mindful tasks.

Below are some examples of tasks where you might want to use the TASK method in order to help you gain the most from the experience:

- studying

- exercising

- eating

- cooking

- driving

- gardening

- listening to music

- journaling

- cleaning your house

- painting

- playing an instrument

- talking to a friend

- going for a walk

- getting ready in the morning

- fixing up an old item

- reorganizing a cluttered closet

- redoing your closets organization system

- rearranging furniture

- having a conversation with a relative

- sewing something

- fixing a shoe

- painting a room

- decorating your apartment

- doing the dishes

- deep cleaning the bathroom

- detailing your car

- reading a book

- listening to an audiobook

What are some other activities you can add into your routine to practice mindfully? Come up with your own and use the TASK method to complete them with mindfulness.

Exercise: Mindfulness Core Skills Calendar

When you are mindful, it's important to note this time along with any sensations that come alone. What skill was used to keep you mindful? Along with the skill, it's also helpful to track whether or not this was difficult, if there was an emotional release, and whether or not you experienced resistance when participating in this skill.

Below is an example of how you can keep track of these mindful moments. Noting mindfulness in happy or productive moments is just as important as noticing when you're mindful after experiencing stress.

Day	Skill	Difficulty	Release	Resistance
Monday	Mindful cooking and meal prepping dinners for the week.	5/10	8/10	At first it was hard to focus and I felt overwhelmed, but after the first 20 minutes, it was much easier to get lost in what I was doing.
Tuesday	Identifying five senses while waiting for my pickup order.	3/10	7/10	It was easy to focus since I was feeling slightly anxious, but mostly bored as I waited for my order to be ready.
Wednesday	Mindful nature walk.	8/10	10/10	I really didn't want to leave my house at first, but once I finally put on my walking shoes to go, I was able to focus on nature and pay attention to my senses.

Use the empty chart below to help you keep track of the mindfulness skills you displayed throughout the week. After you've filled out the chart for the week, pay attention to what changes you might be able to make in the future to reduce mindfulness difficulty and resistance.

Day	Skill	Difficulty	Release	Resistance
Monday	1. 2. 3.	1. 2. 3.	1. 2. 3.	1. 2. 3.
Tuesday	1. 2. 3.	1. 2. 3.	1. 2. 3.	1. 2. 3.
Wednesday	1. 2. 3.	1. 2. 3.	1. 2. 3.	1. 2. 3.
Thursday	1. 2. 3.	1. 2. 3.	1. 2. 3.	1. 2. 3.
Friday	1. 2. 3.	1. 2. 3.	1. 2. 3.	1. 2. 3.

Saturday	1. 2. 3.	1. 2. 3.	1. 2. 3.	1. 2. 3.
Sunday	1. 2. 3.	1. 2. 3.	1. 2. 3.	1. 2. 3.

Exercise: Participate

To participate in something means to fully immerse yourself in that experience. For this exercise, try three different activities that you can participate in. This should involve one thing you dislike, one thing that you enjoy, and one thing that you feel neutral or indifferent about. Examples include:

Enjoyable Activities	Neutral Activities	Non-Enjoyable Activities
Watching TV	Putting away clean dishes	Paying bills
Eating	Taking a shower	Going to the dentist
Going to a concert	Preparing a meal	Mowing the lawn

Use the chart below to help you decipher some activities that you believe are good, neutral, or bad.

Enjoyable Activities	Neutral Activities	Non-Enjoyable Activities

Now, pick one activity from each column and fully participate in that activity. Consider these questions when participating in them, and answer them in a diary after your participation to help you boost your level of engagement the next time:

- Were you able to "become one" with the task at hand?

- How were you able to do this?

- What intuitive feelings did you have while participating?

- What is a way that you can increase your participation in the future?

- What was your overall experience?

- How might you describe this experience to a friend?

- Whas this a memorable experience?

- What senses were involved in the process?

- What senses did you feel as you endured everything that happened?

- What forms of resistance arose that made it difficult to complete this activity?

- What other forms of encouragement were present that helped you finish the activity with ease?

Overview: Mindfulness

There are five main skills to remember when cultivating mindfulness:

1. observation

2. sensation

3. judgment

4. neutrality

5. participation

To be mindful requires that you are observant. Identify objective characteristics of the space around you. Notice what creates and exists within the space, and pay attention to your sensations. Use your body to help you notice what happens in every scenario, and always withhold judgment. You can exist by making assumptions or requiring reason. Staying neutral gives you more autonomy over your emotions, making it easier for you to fully participate in the life happening around you. After learning how to be mindful, you increased awareness of your emotions, leading to enhanced emotional regulation.

Chapter 3

——————⌃——————

Emotional Regulation

AWARENESS IS A GOOD START, but as we unpack our emotions, it's important to next understand how to regulate those thoughts and feelings.

Everyone has emotions. Sometimes the intensity with which we feel those emotions can have a negative impact on our life, so next comes learning how to emotionally regulate to get ahead of our feelings.

You can't always stop unwanted emotions from happening. Unwanted emotions refer to what some might call "negative emotions." It's important to avoid categorizing emotions into either "good" or "bad" categories. Recall neutrality skills from the previous lessons. Unwanted emotions are those that can present as catalysts to bigger issues, including more emotional dysregulation.

Mindfulness helps you identify the emotion, and now regulation is the action of creating stability with these feelings. First, start by fact-checking the situation. Assumptions or triggering feelings can inflate our perception of the scenario.

Once you have reduced the visceral reaction of emotion, you can then name it to create a better awareness of how this feels. Labeling emotions, or naming, is a way to decrease the negative impact of these feelings (Vaughn, n.d-a).

There are many triggers to emotions. These include sights, smells, sounds, and thoughts (*Emotional Regulation*, n.d.). Even after emotions are regulated, outside triggers could cause further disruption, so strong coping skills can be used to prevent you from falling into an unwanted emotional cycle.

Once emotions are identified, and triggers are mediated, the next important skill to flourish is responding to that emotion. Two people experiencing the same emotion can respond in opposite ways. Responses can cause emotions to inflate, but when regulated, proper emotional responses assist in overall management.

Emotional management allows you to use past experiences to ensure that you don't keep repeating the same emotional cycles.

Fact-Checking

Is what you are feeling true, or do these false senses create fears from trauma or past experiences? Believing the false things we say about ourselves can lead to a cycle of negative thinking. Your mind is very imaginative, which means it's easy to create endless scenarios that are untrue and serve no productive purpose. Instead, these false scenarios can trick our mind into believing in a different reality versus what is objectively true. While you can't ever know someone's true opinion or feelings, you can know the objective facts of a situation. These are the main factors to focus on when our emotions are causing confusion in relation to how we should act properly.

Examples of scenarios when you might use fact-checking skills:

- A cryptic text from a friend makes you wonder if they're mad at you.

- You feel the urge to cancel a date because you're not feeling good about your appearance.

- You stay quiet during a party out of fear of judgment from others.

- You assume you're not performing well at work based on a few passive and mostly neutral comments your boss made.

Fact-checking is always helpful when we feel lost in the endless possibilities that lie ahead. There's no way to predict the future or change the past, so managing our emotions based on facts will ensure we continue to live mindfully.

Exercise: Emotional Tracking

Tracking your emotions is a great way to objectively identify what you are feeling when you are feeling it. This will then help you discover the "who," "why," and "how" of understanding and managing that emotion. Below is a simple method that you can use to make this emotional tracking much easier. Identify the time, and following, complete the sentence on the line provided:

- Time:__:____: I am feeling _____

- Time:__:____: I am feeling _____

- Time:__:____: I am feeling _____

- Time:__:____: I am feeling _____

- Time:__:____: I am feeling _____

- Time:__:____: I am feeling _____

- Time:__:____: I am feeling _____

- Time:__:____: I am feeling _____

- Time:__:____: I am feeling _____

- Time:__:____: I am feeling _____

- Time:__:____: I am feeling _____

- Time:__:____: I am feeling _____

- Time:__:____: I am feeling _____

- Time:__:____: I am feeling _____

- Time:__:____: I am feeling _____

- Time:__:____: I am feeling _____

- Time:__:____: I am feeling _____

- Time:__:____: I am feeling _____

- Time:__:____: I am feeling _____

- Time:__:____: I am feeling _____

- Time:__:____: I am feeling _____

After keeping track of this for a few days, you can then start to break down what those emotions mean, helping you to investigate all the ways they've been affecting your behavior. This analysis can be done using the **REST** method:

- Response: How did you react?

- Evoke: What other feelings did this evoke?

- Trigger: What was the trigger of the emotion?

- Side effects: What happened after your response?

- Once you identify these four parts of your recorded feelings, you can then allow yourself to rest as the side effects subside. Below is an example chart you can use to help you breakdown your feelings:

Feeling	Response	Evoke	Trigger	Side Effects
Excitement	Shared this feeling with others	Happiness Nervousness Feeling at ease	Upcoming vacation	It was easier to concentrate and get work done
Content	N/A	Peace Tranquility Acceptance	Laying on the couch watching TV	N/A - I was able to simply enjoy my night off
Anger	Started a fight with friend	Annoyance Rage Offense	Friend was upset I had to cancel plans	I couldn't focus on my tasks because I was worried about the fight.
Overwhelmed	Walked away and did some deep breathing	Panic Dread Exhaustion	Having too many things to do	At first I felt more emotions, but by walking away, I was able to calm down.

Use the empty chart below to fill out your own:

Feeling	Response	Emotion	Trigger	Side Effects

Exercise: Check the Facts

When the mind starts running, it's easy to get lost in the current of the endless stream of thoughts. Instead of getting trampled by these fears, regrets, and other unwanted emotions, you can use fact-checking to see if your fears are a reality. Below is a chart explaining how you can check the facts when feeling anxious. Use the three I's to help you investigate whether or not you are following truth or fear.

Example situation: You're panicked because you've just got a speeding ticket in the mail. Money is already tight, and you don't know how you're going to pay for it. You can't help but ruminate and worry.

Immediate	Intensity	Imagination
Highlight what immediacy/danger is present in the situation: Threat	Highlight what intense emotion you feel, or write your own: Fear	Highlight which aspect of your imagination is being activated in this moment: Guess

Loss	Anger	Assumption
Harm	_____	Comparison
Describe this immediacy: Fear of the loss of income, or losing driving privileges for too many speeding tickets.	Describe this intensity: Fear over what is going to happen, anger at self for speeding, worry and anxiety over how this is going to affect the future.	Describe this imagination: Assuming the worst is going to happen, and envisioning these scenarios.

Use the empty chart below to help you check the facts:

Immediate	Intensity	Imagination
Highlight what immediacy/danger is present in the situation: Threat Loss	Highlight what intense emotion you feel, or write your own: Fear Anger	Highlight which aspect of your imagination is being activated in this moment: Guess Assumption

Harm	_____	Comparison
_____	_____	_____
Describe this immediacy:	Describe this intensity:	Describe this imagination:

Exercise: New Perspective

Look to your left. Now look to your right. If two different people only had access to one side, what would they think about your space?

Perspective determines how we respond emotionally and behaviorally to a situation. Shifting perspectives can help you gain new insight into the things that impact your mindset the most.

For this exercise, think of a recent situation that upset you. Then, fill in the empty chart to help you see how this situation can have multiple perspectives. Below is an example chart to get you started:

Example situation: You recently met someone, and the two of you really hit it off. You exchanged numbers and have been texting almost nonstop since. Recently, you said something that they had a strong reaction to. Now, you haven't heard from them in a few hours, even though you text mostly all day.

Focal Point	Backstory	Timeline	Intention
From your perspective, you are focused on the situation that they had a strong reaction to. You are feeling regretful and worried now because you don't know if you did and said the wrong thing.	The backstory is the two of you's relationship: you have been texting nonstop, so that serves as evidence that now, something is different.	Your perspective is based on the timeline you are focusing on. On one hand, the timeline might be focused simply on the last few months, since the two of you have met.	What is the intention behind this perspective? From your perspective, you are intended on fixing the situation and determining if the other person is upset with you.
Now, think of it from the focal point of the other person. Perhaps they are working late and don't have time to respond.	Their backstory might be that they were feeling overwhelmed by the constant texting, and now they want to take a break to focus on work. They like you, but they want to take some time to respond before the situation becomes more intense.	Their timeline is focused on how they haven't been performing well at work, and they want to ensure they stay on track so their performance keeps improving, rather than getting worse.	Their intention is to focus on themselves right now. It's not that they don't care about you; they will text back later. Right now, in this moment, and in their timeline, they need to pay attention to work rather than texting.

Shifting perspectives can help you see yourself outside of the problem. It's easy to assume you did something wrong, and now bad things will happen, especially when our perspective frames things in this way. However, by shifting perspectives, you can see that the situation isn't centered on you and there are many other factors at play. Use the empty chart below to help you shift perspectives on a situation that recently left lingering feelings of anxiety.

Focal Point	Backstory	Timeline	Intention

Naming

Naming your emotions will give you a better sense of what these feelings look like. Ascribing an identity to an emotion makes it easier to figure out, therefore assisting in the emotional management process.

Examples of scenarios when you might use naming skills:

- You can't seem to work or focus, and you're not sure why.

- Your partner is arguing with you, and you're struggling to see the bigger issue.

- A small joke with a friend turned into a heated argument.

- You keep getting caught up on a past conversation you had with a friend.

- You feel stuck inside with work and want to take the day off to hang out with friends.

Naming emotions is something that should happen when you're in a good mood, just as often as when you're dealing with unwanted emotions. Waiting until you're in a bad mood to practice emotional management can lead you to associate emotions in general with a negative connotation. When you are feeling happy, excited, hopeful, and peaceful, take note of what this emotion looks like and what different names you can assign to it.

Exercise: Describing Emotions

To help assist in the emotional naming process, consider creating a character for each emotion. When a writer creates a story, they must consider many different elements to help them come up with someone believable, relatable, and realistic. Below is a chart you can use to help in the naming process. By attributing different qualities to emotions, you can recognize what they look like when they arise in your life. The first emotion is filled out for you. Use the empty spaces to fill out the rest.

Emotion	Character Traits	Actions Associated	Descriptive Words
Anger	Quick to react, uses violence or passive aggressiveness, causes chaos.	Screaming, yelling, throwing things, hitting people.	Red, loud explosive sounds, sweating and tense muscles.

Another method you can use to describe emotions is an emotion chain. Our emotions often interlink with each other, creating not just a singular feeling but a chain of multiple emotions. For example, fear might turn into insecurity, which could lead to feelings of helplessness. To help you familiarize yourself with more emotions, fill in the blanks below. What other emotions would you add to these chains? Add even more emotions after the provided lines if you think of additional links in the chain. The first one is filled out for you.

- angry

- sad

- happy

- afraid

- stunned

- proud

- nervous

- disgusted

- hurt

- _____

- _____

- _____

- _____

- _____

- _____

- _____

- _____

- _____

- _____

- _____

- _____

- _____

- _____

- _____

- _____

Exercise: Primary and Secondary Emotions

Primary emotions are the instant feelings you have and what can be identified in relation to the core, underlying emotions. Secondary emotions are what follows. By building the skill of labeling emotions, you will make better sense of the things you're feeling. When we group emotions into limited categories, it means repeating the same behavioral pattern in association with how that made us initially feel. Breaking down feelings allows you to see more intricacies in how you are feeling, which will assist in changing behavior. For example, you might get angry with your partner. By identifying that you are actually frustrated and feeling neglected, you can find solutions to discuss this with your partner rather than acting on feelings of anger.

Below is a chart of primary emotions with a list of secondary emotions that can break down those feelings. Beneath the existing ones, fill in some words that you associate with the primary emotion.

Primary	Secondary
Anger	Rage
	Hatred
	Frustration
	Offended
	Annoyance
Fear	Anxiety
	Worry
	Disappointment
	Offended
	Panic
Sadness	Misery
	Hopelessness
	Let down
	Helpless
	Grieving

Happiness	Joy
	Cheerful
	Relieved
	Confident
	Fulfilled
Excited	Overwhelmed
	Jubilated
	Exhilarated
	Surprised
	Elated

Now, use the chart below to help you fill in the five emotions that you feel the most in the primary column. These might differ from the ones above, or they might be the same. Whenever you label an emotion, return to the chart to add in your own secondary emotions in relation to the primary. The more words you have to describe feelings, the easier it will be to recognize when you're experiencing it to act accordingly.

Primary	Secondary

Exercise: Emotional Purpose

Every machine has a purpose. It's created with a specific intent, following a set of rules to meet objectives. Some machines are built differently, and many work in various ways. The one thing they all hold true is that they were originally crafted in order to fulfill a basic need.

A computer is built to help you access digital documents, games, and the internet. A can opener was built to open tin cans. An oven was built to cook.

When you are trying to make better sense of your emotions, you can start by focusing on the reason your body is following that emotional pattern. There's a reason your body is sending you the signal. There's an underlying influence over the specifics that created this emotion. Now you are experiencing the feelings and other side effects that come along without knowing that purpose. Something inside of you is missing or needs attention.

You can't figure out emotions to the exact characteristic that creates them. However, you can give yourself a basic understanding of what the purpose that emotion is trying to tell you. It's usually either going to give you a specific need, a warning, a reminder, or it might simply arise because of natural triggers around you. When thinking about machines, look at what is happening internally. Something like a computer has covers. You don't see all the exposed hard drives and wires that are built into the computer.

Look at the closest machine around you. Think about the covers that are over the machine and what is happening inside, behind the metal plates. Remember to consider the purpose and what this machine was initially created for.

How does that emotion appear to others? After the fact, you can also determine if this emotion served its purpose.

This is a visual way to see your emotion physically, to help you at least have a sense of the basic operating system. Not everybody knows how a microwave works or what scientific explanation there is for the phenomenon that occurs. But we do know how to put something in the microwave and hit the numbers to make it reheat our food.

This is the basic understanding that you need to have of your emotions in order to help you determine whether or not they're serving their purpose or providing you with a need. Trying to figure out the complexities of every emotion that you have is impossible. Your brain is not a microwave—it's much more complicated than that. There's a balance between having a basic understanding of what you're feeling and what that emotion is trying to do versus over-analyzing your emotions to the point that you are ruminating and overthinking.

Coping

Naming and understanding emotions doesn't make them go away, so healthy coping skills can increase our ability to deal with feelings. When triggers pop up, or you start to lose feelings of control, coping skills can assist with the reduction of unwanted emotions.

Examples of scenarios when you might use coping skills:

- The way a customer talks to you at work triggers intense emotions.

- You're feeling the urge to self-harm.

- A sight or smell suddenly triggers you when you're out in public.

- You are running late for work and want to skip the day as you feel a panic attack rising.

Coping with intense emotions is a crucial skill so that even after you've started the regulation process, you're prepared for any emotions that lie ahead.

Exercise: TIPP

Some emotions are so intense that we need to have immediate coping mechanisms ready so as to prevent these emotions from negatively influencing us. A DBT coping mechanism to use is known as the TIPP acronym (Rosenthal, n.d.). This stands for :

T: temperature

I: intense exercise

P: pace your breathing

P: paired muscle relaxation

Whenever you feel panic arising, you can follow these four steps to help you calm down and relax. This is also a good rule of thumb to remember with regular emotional coping and can help you reduce unwanted emotions in the long-term when practiced consistently. Follow the example activities in the chart below when you are in need of a coping mechanism:

Temperature	Intense Exercise	Pace Your Breathing	Paired Muscle Relaxation
Stick your face in the freezer. Step outside when it's too hot indoors. Hold an ice cube. Drink a cold glass of water. Turn a fan on and sit in front of it. Take a cold shower. Add your own: _____ _____	Go for a walk. Lift weights. Deep clean a hard to reach area. Cycle for 20 minutes. Climb a set of stairs. Do push-ups. Dance for 20 minutes. Add your own: _____ _____	Practice nose mouth breathing. Practice alternate nostril breathing. Practice guided meditation. Lay down until breathing is regulated. Add your own: _____ _____	Use a massage gun. Self-massage your arm or leg. Take a hot shower. Soak in a hot tub. Tense and then release your muscles. Add your own: _____ _____

Exercise: Mindful Emotion Awareness

Emotional awareness doesn't just occur in the moment. Being mindful of your emotions is something that can be done over time and by reflecting on past experiences just as much as emotions in the present. In fact, looking back, you might notice emotions that you weren't able to identify at the time. The more you build emotional awareness, the easier it will be to make sense of the inspiring factors behind the way you feel. The charts below are activities that you can try in order to help you make more sense of the things you've been feeling in the past and present, therefore increasing awareness in the future.

Instructions: Think of a situation in relation to each of the five prompts. Fill out the corresponding chart based on these four aspects:

- **Immediate response:** What happened right after the emotion? Did you say something you didn't mean or act in a way that you regret? Think back on the immediate feelings, thoughts, and actions that occurred instantly.

- **Memorable effects:** What lingering aspects occurred after this feeling? Did it inspire other emotions, or did it drive you to act in a certain way? Did it cause issues in relationships, or does it continue to affect you to this day?

- **Following response:** What response do you feel at this moment? Does the emotion trigger other feelings? Do you feel a twinge of regret? Are you happy with how you responded?

- **Noticed coping techniques:** Did you notice a method of self-soothing, or a potentially harmful coping mechanism that you partook in after this initial emotion?

By identifying these four parts, you can determine the behavioral effects of your emotions.

Situation: An emotion experienced in the past month. Describe the situation below:

Immediate Response	Memorable Effects	Following Response	Noticed Coping Techniques

Situation: An emotion experienced in the past year. Describe the situation below:

Immediate Response	Memorable Effects	Following Response	Noticed Coping Techniques

Situation: An emotion experienced in the past five years. Describe the situation below:

_____

_____

_____

_____

_____

_____

Immediate Response	Memorable Effects	Following Response	Noticed Coping Techniques

Situation: An emotion experienced as a teenager. Describe the situation below:

_____

_____

_____

_____

_____

_____

Immediate Response	Memorable Effects	Following Response	Noticed Coping Techniques

Situation: An emotion experienced as a child. Describe the situation below:

_____

_____

_____

_____

_____

_____

Immediate Response	Memorable Effects	Following Response	Noticed Coping Techniques

Exercise: Coping Affirmations

Positive affirmations are phrases of optimism that can be added to your vocabulary. You might've heard of them before. They include phrases like, "I am good enough, I am smart, or I am successful."

These can feel a little awkward at first, especially when we are in the middle of a panic attack and can feel anxiety rising. One method to help you realistically reduce intense emotions is through the use of coping affirmations.

These take a more neutral stance to help you find a place of safety and peace when your emotions are scary. Try to think of some coping affirmations on your own, and write them down in a journal or on your phone's notes app so you always have them with you. Below are examples of coping affirmations that you can add to your everyday vocabulary:

- I am safe.

- I am protected.

- I am living in harmony.

- I am exactly where I'm supposed to be.

- No one is judging me at this moment.

- No one is thinking my worst thoughts.

- I do not need to do anything at this moment.

- I am capable.

- I am fine.

- Everything is okay.

- Everything will turn out fine.

- I am deserving.

- I am human.

- I am a person with my own thoughts.

- Everyone's experience is different.

- I do not need to have all the answers.

- Nothing is required of me at this moment.

- Others understand me even when it doesn't feel that way.

- I am surrounded by support.

- I will make it through dark times.

- I always come out fine after challenges.

- I was built to overcome adversity.

- I have strong intuition.

- I know how to listen to my body.

- I understand what it means to sit with my emotions.

- The only thing I have to do at this moment is feel what I'm feeling.

- I know what the right thing to do is.

- I make mistakes.

- I overcame my mistakes.

- I am not the mistakes I've made.

- Peace is real.

- I will find peace soon.

- I have gratitude for the peace that surrounds me.

- I will be fine no matter what.

- Everything will work out the way it is supposed to.

- I am resilient.

- I am adaptable.

- I am open to change.

- I welcome new experiences.

- I will always find a way to learn.

- I know what is best for myself.

- I will find a solution.

- There is an answer to all of my questions.

- I trust in life.

- I trust in the process.

- I am patient through the process.

- The past does not define me.

- A singular moment cannot define me.

- Others rarely notice my faults.

- I pay more attention to my faults than others will.

- My worst thoughts are not true.

- My scariest fears will not happen.

- I can't predict the future.

- I can't know for certain how things will turn out.

- I am built to last through the chaos.

- I have experience overcoming obstacles.

- I have meaning.

- I have a purpose.

- I deserve to be here.

- I deserve what good things I have and more.

- I know what peace feels like.

- I know what happiness feels like.

Response

The instance of an emotion has three steps: feeling, reaction, and response. Knowing the difference between these important parts will ensure that you do not cast judgment for the feeling, and you take action on your response.

Examples of scenarios when you might use response skills:

- A friend tells you good news, and you can't help but feel a little jealous.

- Your favorite sports team just lost, and you want to punch a hole in the wall.

- Your partner picks a fight on a road trip, and it's starting to sour the day.

- You stub your toe, causing your coffee to spill all over you.

Every emotion we acknowledge will have a response, no matter how big or small. Regulation relies on knowing the difference between your reaction and response and following suit in a way that facilitates productive behavior.

Exercise: React vs. Respond

Our reaction is our reptilian brain, and a response is based on a conscious choice (*Responding Rather Than Reacting*, n.d.).

Your reaction is the thing that exists naturally in your wiring. It taps into a survival tactic. Your response is what has been learned and practiced over time. Your reaction is mostly out of your control. You can't help it if you're frightened by a spider dropping onto your lap while driving down the highway; that is only natural. Your response might be to panic and veer off the road, or perhaps you are able to keep your cool as you slowly remove the spider from your car. Your response isn't entirely in your control, either. Some of us are taught to respond with fear or rage based on what we witnessed growing up. Mental illnesses can also exacerbate unwanted emotions, leading to various impulsive responses and urges. Use the chart below to help you understand the different ways that you can respond to a situation. The first few are filled out for you. Fill out the remainder with your own situation or triggers:

Situation or Trigger	Reactive Feeling	Response 1	Response 2	Response 3
Favorite sports team loses	Anger	Throwing the remote at the TV and breaking it	Yelling an expletive and walking away	Showing gratitude for an exciting and intense game
A parent refuses to acknowledge trauma inflicted	Neglect, hurt	Telling them they are a terrible parent	Sharing how they have been hurt in childhood	
Two friends are fighting and putting you in the middle	Overwhelmed, frustrated, split in half	Giving both the silent treatment until they work it out		
A partner reveals they have been having an emotional affair	Betrayal, confusion, grief			
An upcoming job interview for a high-paying position has been scheduled				

Exercise: New Reactions

This exercise is now going to aim to take those responses that you filled out and use them to fill out the chart below to help you see the outcome of your reactions. You should have 15 responses in total. Knowing the outcome will help with impulsive decision-making in the moment. The first few are filled out for you, but take some time to write in the previous responses with various potential outcomes:

Response	Outcome
Throwing the remote at the TV and breaking it	This response rooted in anger results in a broken television. The emotion was released, but at the cost of a pricey electronic device. This also ruined the rest of the night of those who witnessed this emotional reaction.
Yelling an expletive and walking away	This was an emotional release, but at least no expensive equipment was sacrificed in the process. However, it did make others who were around feel uncomfortable and changed the vibe of the sports watching party.

Showing gratitude for an exciting and intense game	This response had the quickest outcome. The game ended, but the party carried on, and everyone was able to have a good night together.
Telling them they are a terrible parent	Yelling at a parent can create defensiveness, and rather than hearing the child out, they are more likely to find reasons for justification for their actions.
Sharing how they have been hurt in childhood	While the parent might not listen, the child still did what they could to try and show the parent how they have been hurt overtime.
Giving both the silent treatment until they work it out	This could have multiple outcomes: First, the friends might eventually make up, but it could also lead to more conflict. Alternatively, all three friends might simply stop talking to each other, three friendships ended.

After you've filled out the chart, go back through and reassess some of these outcomes. Was this the best possible outcome? Which ones were most desirable? In the future, when you are trying to work through conflict or responding to a reaction, you can recall the potential outcomes of potential responses. This ensures you are doing the best thing you can at the time, aiming for a positive, helpful, and preferred outcome.

Exercise: Opposite Action

Think back to the exercise about finding the purpose behind your emotion. Biologically, you have these emotions wired into your anatomy to help you take action. Fear tells you to tense up and look around to make sure everything's fine. In the wild, we used to use this when we were walking through the woods, foraging for our food. If a bear starts approaching or we feel the eyes of a tiger or a lion, we tend to stop and raise awareness. This fear emotion had an action that naturally followed in order to help us survive. In modern times, we live much differently, and that means we experience our emotions much differently. Despite our circumstances, biologically, we are similarly wired to how we used to be thousands of years ago. What this means is that you have a stress response wired into you, and that can cause some really complex emotions in today's world. Getting a reminder that your bill is past due or notification about a stressful work email can cause the same biological fears we had when we were looking through the woods thousands of years ago.

One DBT skill to consider is opposite action. This means following the urge and natural response to your emotion and doing the exact opposite, once it comes time to take action. Some examples are below:

When you're angry and you want to call somebody a name, instead, give them a compliment. When you are feeling tired and like you want to skip work for the day, go to work and give 200%.

When you are feeling insecure, want to change back into sweatpants, and skip going out that night, wear your boldest outfit and go out and be your best self.

Following the opposite action as an exercise can make it easier to challenge yourself to take a bold step rather than following a desire to feel shame and hide.

Below are a few more examples of situations where you can use the opposite action, including the emotion that they bring on, what the natural action is, and what the opposite action is going to be.

The first chart is filled out for you, but fill in the rest of the charts based on opposite action, expected action, and emotion.

Situation	You get into an argument with a passive-aggressive coworker who insults your recent project.
Emotion	Anger, hurt, insulted, and frustrated.
Expected Action	Insult them back, getting into a more heated argument.
Opposite Action	Thank them for their criticism and compliment their skills.

Situation	The hotel staff lost your reservation and now you don't have a room for the night.
Emotion	
Expected Action	
Opposite Action	

Situation	You come home after a long day at work to find that the house is a total mess, even though your partner/roommate had the day off with plenty of time to clean.
Emotion	
Expected Action	
Opposite Action	

Use the empty charts below to come up with your own situations, or reflect on past situations where following the opposite action would've been more helpful in the long run.

Situation	
Emotion	
Expected Action	
Opposite Action	

Situation	
Emotion	

Expected Action	
Opposite Action	

Situation	
Emotion	
Expected Action	
Opposite Action	

Management

Managing emotions also means making yourself less vulnerable to feeling these things in the future. Getting through the emotion first is crucial, but next, you have to learn how to archive the situation for future reflection. Repeating the same unwanted emotional cycles means that you are failing to manage them even though you understand how to pull yourself from that situation. Management relies on dedication and accountability from you to want to make improvements.

Emotional management skills should be used regularly. These can be incorporated into a daily, weekly, or monthly routine so you can ensure you stay on track with how you're feeling.

Exercise: Weekly Emotional Calendar

For this next exercise, follow a weekly emotional calendar. You can simply start on whatever day it is now, or you can wait for the next upcoming Sunday to start. There are two charts below.

The first is an example weekly emotional calendar based on the template. The second is an empty calendar for you to use for yourself. You can also consider using a specific color to fill in the square for that day, correlating to a specific emotion. For example, anger might be shades of red, and happiness might be shades of yellow.

An example of a weekly emotional calendar:

Time	Mon.	Tues.	Wed.	Thurs.	Fri.	Sat.	Sun.
12-4 a.m.	anxious	anxious	n/a - sleeping	n/a - sleeping	anxious	anxious	n/a - sleeping
4-8 a.m.	n/a - sleeping	restless	n/a - sleeping	n/a - sleeping	n/a - sleeping	n/a - sleeping	n/a - sleeping
8 a.m. - 12 p.m.	nervous/rushed	busy	tired	focused	focused	peaceful	happy
12-4 p.m.	content	busy	annoyed	focused	excited	happy	stressed
4-8 p.m.	tired	rushed	relaxed	relaxed	content	content	anxious
8 p.m. -12 a.m.	anxious	n/a - sleeping	relaxed	n/a - sleeping	excited	excited	anxious

As you can see, if the entirety of the four hours were spent sleeping, those blocks were skipped. Other than that, one or two words were used to help summarize the overall emotions of that period. You can then go back through and identify certain patterns that arose throughout the week. It seemed that the person this chart belonged to was feeling rushed and overwhelmed early in the week and late at night. They felt the most relaxed and peaceful toward the weekend. They were able to be focused toward the end of the week. After reviewing a schedule like this, the person might then be able to come up with ideas on how to maximize the productive emotions and minimize, reduce, or prevent the unwanted emotions that present challenges.

Now, use the empty chart below to track your emotions.

Time	Mon.	Tues.	Wed.	Thurs.	Fri.	Sat.	Sun.
12-4 a.m.							
4-8 a.m.							
8 a.m. -12 p.m.							
12-4 p.m.							
4-8 p.m.							
8 p.m. -12 a.m.							

Exercise: Smiles and Hands

Your body will communicate to your mind how you are feeling (Lineham, 2015).

When you're sitting with your shoulders slumped and your head down, that's going to tell your mind that you are not feeling like your best self. What you can do is pull your shoulders back to feel more confident. Small changes in our body can be very effective in changing your mood.

One exercise to follow is the smiles and hand exercise. Our faces and hands are arguably the most communicable sources of us. Our faces express what we need. We show our emotions through the way that we hold our eyes, cheeks, nose, lips, tongue, and teeth.

When you're feeling stressed out, overwhelmed, and you can't think or focus, stand in front of the mirror and pay attention to how you're using your mind and your hands. Relax your face, let all the tension leave your brow, forehead, nose, cheeks, and mouth.

Don't hold any tenseness in your smile, and slightly turn the corners of your mouth. Move that relaxation down to your shoulders and relax your elbows, thumbs, and your hands. Keep them unclenched flat, and notice any tension or urge to make a fist as it rises. Whenever you are feeling stressed or overwhelmed, notice the way that your face and hands are because this is going to communicate to your body and those around you how you feel.

This exercise is one you can include in your morning routine. Waking up and giving a slight smile might just be enough to boost your mood. When you feel stressed, unclench your fist and place your hand flat. Relax your face and shoulders. You might still feel anxious, but these small actions are ways to chip away at powerful emotions.

Overview: Emotional Regulation

There are five main skills to remember when improving emotional regulation:

1. fact-checking

2. naming

3. coping

4. response

5. management

Emotions are powerful, but they aren't always factual. They can tell us important things we might need to know about ourselves, however, so naming them will give you the power to figure out what they might be trying to say. Once you learn how to identify emotions, you can then add coping mechanisms to keep your responses productive and helpful. This process together creates a strong level of emotional regulation. Even with practice, however, we are not entirely free from intense, rapidly occurring, and overpowering emotions. Knowing distress tolerance skills will keep you level-headed no matter what situation you might find yourself in.

Chapter 4

Distress Tolerance

PREVENTING AND RECOVERING FROM emotions is an important part of mental health management, but what do you do when you're in the middle of a crisis? Distress can cause excess emotional and physical pain. Knowing how to make it through a crisis will reduce suffering.

This starts by stopping the emotion. From the moment you are able to name or identify the emotion, stopping ensures that you can begin the reduction of unwanted feelings. This prevents escalation.

Providing distraction is a good way to pause side effects while your body cools down and your mind settles. This is also important for stopping emotions that you acknowledge are rising rather than waiting until after they've peaked.

Self-soothing is another crucial skill for distress tolerance, as this ensures you don't seek outside measures to soothe. Looking for external validation or numbing methods can lead to substance abuse or dependency issues. Providing yourself with inner reassurance enables you to have a solid support system in your own mind.

Radical acceptance is the best way to find a place of neutrality, furthering preventative measures from labeling scenarios as being either good or bad. This type of commitment will be further explored in the radical acceptance skills section.

During a time of vulnerability, empowering oneself assists in the reduction of distress, increasing tolerance for the future. Those who are struggling with distress might feel "stuck and out of control (*Survive a Crisis*, 2019). Self-empowerment gives that control back when you maintain practice with empowerment skills.

Stopping

When in crisis, the first thing to do is to stop and think to prevent the emotions from making the situation worse. Emotions can be very powerful, so fighting when you're already stressed can make conflict worse. Making impulsive decisions when you're feeling depressed can add more problems to a situation. Knowing how to cool down and walk away is the first important step.

Examples of scenarios when you might use stopping skills:

- Someone picks a fight at a bar after a night of heavy drinking.

- Your child refuses to go to sleep and keeps throwing tantrums.

- You get cut off in traffic.

- After returning home with your takeout order, you realize the restaurant forgot one of your side dishes.

When sudden disruptions in our expectations change, it can cause heated emotions to come on fast. No matter how big or small the grievance, any sort of daily annoyance is enough to spark a series of frustrating events. Identifying red-flag feelings and using the STOP (stop, take a step back, observe, and proceed mindfully) acronym should be used in times of high distress.

Exercise: Red-Flag Feelings

Red flag feelings can be defined as emotions which lead to destructive or out-of-control behaviors and actions (Brantley et al., 2007). Just by reading the first sentence, you likely have a few scenarios in mind when you hear the word "destructive behavior." Whether this means the destruction of physical property, or damage to a relationship, there might still be lingering effects of your heightened emotional state.

High emotions make it hard for us to be able to take the right action. Instead, we are driven by deep urges, which can sometimes make us want to hurt others. Anger driven by fear can cause us to quickly and impulsively act. When you feel the urge to become defensive or angry, you might physically attack or wish to harm others.

When high emotions are in the driver's seat, it can lead to feelings of rage, vengefulness, retaliation, revenge, and other impulsive feelings. You might feel the urge to "win" or put others down. You might want to embarrass or belittle someone, especially after feeling personally attacked by them. When these situations and deep urges arise, you can label them as red flag feelings.

You can also identify red-flag feelings by how they make you feel. If an emotion is making you want to isolate, self-harm, or take your rage out on your surroundings (like punching a wall), this can also be a sign to cool down.

Remember that red flag feelings aren't just those that cause distress. They can also lead to feelings of deep hopelessness and despair. The urge to quit a project that you started or skip an important class might be connected to the fear of failure. Depressive symptoms are red flags that your body might be trying to tell you to stop, slow down, and collect yourself.

To identify red-flag feelings, first, think of what makes you feel red. What clouds your judgment and gets in the way of decision-making? What makes you feel red and hot? What makes you feel flushed or embarrassed? What makes your heart start pounding?

Now, take a moment to list these feelings. Write them down below:

Identify three or more red-flags for each emotion. Consider the thoughts, physical feelings, and secondary emotions. You can use the chart below. A few are filled in for you, but use the rest to add in your own emotions and red flags.

Emotion	Red Flag #1	Red Flag #2	Red Flag #3
Grief	Hopelessness	Lethargy	Denial
Panic	Fast heart beat	Blurry vision	
Terror	Shaking		
Ecstasy			

In addition, use these prompts to help you discover some of the feelings that might be considered red flag:

- What is an emotion that instantly gets you fired up?

- What unwanted emotion do you struggle with the most?

- What emotion caused your last regret?

- What is one emotion you wish you felt less?

- What instantly makes your blood boil?

- What makes you so euphoric that it causes you to make poor decisions?

Picture red-flag feelings as your body's alarm system. There is something deep inside of you that you need to address, even if that means just calming down your anger. Focus on listing red-flag feelings first when you are in a neutral mindset to help you fully grasp what you're feeling.

After feeling these red flag emotions, you can then go back and identify what it was that might have led up to these emotions, therefore preventing them from causing further damage in the future.

Exercise: STOP

When dealing with intense emotions, the STOP acronym can help you remember the next four important steps to take (Lineham, 2015):

1. Stop: Before you take any action: stop. This is an important step to follow even when you are in a good mood because it can be easy to be impulsive when emotions are heightened, such as bliss, excitement, or romantic feelings. When emotions are feeling intense, stop what you're doing to determine whether or not the steps you choose to take forward are going to be beneficial overall.

2. Take a Step Back: The next important thing to do is to take a step back. Picture yourself outside of the situation. Look down from a bird's eye perspective. What little things did you miss after your initial and immediate evaluation of the situation? When you are able to take a step back, this means that you have more time to process what is actually going on. In addition, take a step back into the moments leading up to this. Are you tired, hungry, or overwhelmed? Acknowledging the inciting for the heightened emotion can help ensure you're not acting based on triggering events.

3. Observe: Observe the situation around you. What are the underlying factors, influences, or other important pieces to put together in order for you to find the most productive and valuable solution? Observe how others are interacting at the moment. You might be feeding off somebody else's heightened emotions, and the two of you are validating or invalidating each other.

4. Proceed Mindfully: Lastly, proceed mindfully. Once you're able to remove yourself from the situation and gather all of the important aspects that you need to understand the objective standpoint of the situation, you will then be able to proceed in the best way possible. This will ensure that you do not make any destructive or impulsive decisions that you end up regretting later on.

Part of managing your emotions means managing your response and the way in which you choose to proceed. When an emotion starts rising and makes you feel as though you're losing a sense of control, remember to STOP.

Distraction

Not to be confused with avoidance, distraction is necessary during times of increased anxiety. This can give us a temporary waiting period while emotions calm down so that problem-solving skills will be put to better use after the initial emotions have cleared.

Examples of scenarios when you might use distraction skills:

- You're waiting on a text back from someone you've had a crush on.

- Your first day at a new job starts tomorrow, and your stomach is turning.

- You've been struggling with migraines and are awaiting test results from the doctor, causing you to fear the worst.

Distractions are needed when we can't stop thinking about the worst-case scenario. It's easy to envision endless possibilities of all that could turn into a disaster, but this only creates excessive internal emotions with nowhere for that stress to go.

Exercise: Distracting Yourself

Distractions are great ways to keep your mind busy when it doesn't stop spending all of your energy on anxious and ruminating emotions.

When you can't seem to focus on work, it might feel counterintuitive to find a distraction, but what you might discover is that you are able to give your brain a moment to calm down so that you can really focus on the important things that need your attention after you've managed to quiet the mind.

Small activities might only take five minutes, but it could be enough to reset your brain so that you're more focused and concentrated moving forward.

For this activity, fill in the chart below to help you think of different ideas for distractions. Some of the sections have already been filled out with a few examples. It is now your job to go back through and add in more activities. Next time you're feeling anxious, you can refer back to these charts to help you determine what important distractions to try:

Distraction	Examples
Chores: These are great ways to keep you focused on a specific task while also doing something productive.	• Doing dishes • Mopping • Folding laundry

Organization: Any type of organization will help you have something specific to focus on while also counting, which is a great way to focus your mind elsewhere.	• Cleaning out a junk drawer • Going through old socks • Categorizing pictures
Writing/Reading: Reading and writing causes you to focus on the words in front of you while processing specific information, providing a great distraction.	• Journaling • Watching a movie with subtitles • Reading a book

Creativity: When you are creative, your mind is forced to come up with new ideas and dive into different territories of the brain, giving a great distraction.	• Sewing • Painting • Learning an instrument
Household Activities: Aside from chores, having a fun and engaging household activity planned will be a great way to keep you distracted when your thoughts are endlessly running.	• Gardening • Redecorating • Painting a room

Experimentation: Trying something brand new is a jolt of distraction to your brain, providing you with many of the same benefits as the previous distractions listed.	• Baking a new recipe • Watching a new movie • Exploring a new neighborhood in your town
Games/Activities: Games and activities are designed to pull your attention, so it's a good idea to have this type of distraction on hand.	• Puzzles • Video games • Sudoku

Exercise: ACCEPTS

Have you ever been to the doctor's office, nervous about getting a shot or having blood drawn? If so, the nurses might've tried to distract you at the moment. They knew that if your mind was focused elsewhere, you would be less likely to fixate on the pain or fear of the shot and able to work through these challenging emotions. One exercise to help further keep you distracted is the ACCEPTS acronym coined by the DBT founder herself, Marsha Lineham (2015). This stands for:

- activities

- contributing

- comparisons

- emotions

- pushing away

- thoughts

- sensations

As previously discussed, activities are a great starting point. Always start here when you are feeling distracted, anxious, and fixated on certain emotions. But what about when you don't have access to these activities, like if you're at work or somewhere in public? Getting so hyper focused in the moment will make the emotions of fear feel worse, therefore, harder to manage. Next, find contributions.

Helping others is a great distraction. If you are feeling anxious and distracted at a party, ask the host if you can help in any way. They might assign you a simple task that can make you feel helpful and at the very least, distracted. If you are in class, contribute to the discussion by asking questions. Focus on your contribution in the moment when in need of distractions.

Sometimes you can't do anything but sit with your feelings. This is when you can focus on comparisons. Recall periods of distress that you survived. Use these as examples that you are capable of overcoming adversity and making it through even the biggest challenges. Think about the other methods that you could be coping with but aren't. Compare yourself to others who aren't coping, as well as a reminder that you are doing what is needed to stay resilient.

Find something to change your emotional state. For example, if you are stressed, watch a funny video. If you are feeling hopeless, read something inspirational. Try to distract yourself with new emotions to help you overcome the unwanted feelings that are driving your behavior now. Horror movies or suspense thrillers are great distractions because they get our adrenaline pumping. By the time you are finished with a movie or even a short video, you might find that your emotional state is reduced.

Create visual blockades of the situation and picture yourself physically pushing these emotions away. How can you remove them from your life to ensure they don't keep coming back? This is important for times when you can't do anything but sit with your emotions. This will make them feel even more intense because you have no other choice but to ruminate about them. Picture yourself physically pushing them out of the door and then slamming it in their face. Eventually, you can deal with the emotion, but wait until it is reduced or when you're in a more stable place.

Find something to help provide you with distracting thoughts. The best way to do this is to have a conversation with yourself. Find a neutral voice to help evaluate some of the things passing through your mind.

When all else fails, distract your senses. Sniff something fragrant. Change up the temperature. Touch the texture of your jeans. Look in a new direction and focus on what you see. Take a sip of hydrating water. Distracting your senses can help snap your focus in a new direction.

By learning the ACCEPTS foundational skills, you will enable yourself to stay distracted from heightened emotions, allowing you to focus on what's important, and leading yourself to manage the emotions when you're in a different emotional state.

Self-Soothing

Knowing how to calm yourself down and provide inner reassurance during times of distress is important for the instant reduction of dissatisfying emotions.

Examples of scenarios when you might use self-soothing skills:

- Your roommate or partner is gone for the night, and every little noise in the house is making you scared.

- You've been struggling to get out of bed most mornings and feel deep sorrow every day.

- You've been experiencing panic attacks and moments of extreme lethargy.

- You've become fearful of leaving the house and attending social events.

When emotions become too much, it causes us to isolate ourselves. This further drains our energy, making it hard to take care of ourselves in the optimum way that is needed for good health.

Exercise: NEED

When was the last time you were so hungry that it started to affect your emotions? Our bodies have internal signals that remind us to do certain things to fulfill our basic needs. You start yawning, and your eyes get heavy when it's time to go to bed. Your stomach grumbles, and it's hard to concentrate when you're hungry. Your legs get sore, and your body gets restless when you haven't gotten out of the house for a few days.

This next acronym is to remind you how to check in with your basic needs. The acronym is NEED. This stands for:

- nutrition

- energy

- exercise

- doctor

First, look at what you are eating. If you are not giving your body the proper vitamins and nutrients that it needs to function, then you are not going to feel good. Sometimes it is as simple as that. Unfortunately, we live in a society where there's a heavy emphasis on dieting so that your body looks a certain way.

When it comes to fulfilling your basic nutritional needs, forget what you have been taught about eating a certain way based on external factors. What matters most is that you are eating things that provide your body with sustenance. This means fulfilling basic nutritional values like getting calcium, protein, carbohydrates, and different vitamins and minerals necessary for the functioning of your body. It's also important to ensure that you are eating multiple times a day.

In the hustle and bustle of our modern lifestyle, it's easy to skip breakfast and lunch, and then binge eat at dinner time and all throughout the rest of the night. Unfortunately, this isn't the best way to keep your body focused throughout the day. You need carbohydrates, sugars, and proteins to keep your mind functioning. If you struggle with concentrating on work or focusing in class, it might be because you're not giving your body the proper nutrition. Again, it's not about going on a diet and only eating certain types of foods. Focus instead on making sure that you're meeting your bare-minimum nutritional level.

How you choose to do that is completely up to you. If you want to continue to eat certain foods, that's fine. You can supplement with vitamins; however, the body processes foods best when they are eaten as whole foods. For example, if you need more iron in your diet, you can take an iron supplement. However, your body will process iron-rich foods, like beans and legumes, easier than it will an iron supplement. That's not to make you feel bad. It's just to serve as a reminder that you should seek out foods to add nutritional value to your lifestyle and supplement only when needed.

The next letter in the acronym is focused on your energy levels. Again, sometimes your mood is as simple as not getting enough sleep or getting too much sleep. Your body needs about seven to eight hours of sleep a night as an adult. In a later activity, we'll discuss tips for a healthy sleep schedule. However, remember that monitoring your energy level will correlate with your mental health.

This also relies on a certain level of physical activity. Your body takes in a certain number of calories a day, and that energy needs to be used in some way. We burn calories naturally by doing things like walking from place to place, processing the food we ate through digestion, and even sleeping uses up some of our energy. When you are not using that energy that can cause issues with how you feel, which leads us to the next letter of the acronym which stands for exercise.

Everybody needs a certain level of exercise to help keep up with their body's energy levels. For the most part, it's important to get around two and a half hours or more of exercise a week. This can be spread out through very small increments, so you might exercise for 10 minutes multiple times a day. However, you might allocate all your exercising to two or three days a week. Whatever you prefer is up to you, but it is important for you to find small ways to add in more physical movement so that you're using your body's energy and keeping up with a cycle of good health.

You might be thinking to yourself, "I know that I need to do this but how can I actually eat nutritional foods and exercise when my anxiety keeps me in bed?" If you're struggling, it's important to look at the emotional habits that are driving your behavior.

That is what many of these activities are set to do. However, if you're still struggling, and you can't seem to nourish your body, get any good sleep, or have the motivation to exercise, that takes us to the final letter of the acronym which is doctor.

When you are struggling so much that you can't take care of yourself, it is important to seek medical help. Start with your primary care physician. They can run simple tests, check blood work and check your heart and pulse to ensure that everything is functioning as it should. Afterwards, they can then help assess what underlying issues might be causing your struggles, emotionally and physically. The important thing to emphasize about this acronym is that if you're struggling, things won't get better on their own. Start with your basic needs. Strive to follow through with these four things, because that is how change will be possible. While it might feel impossible to even take the step to make a doctor's appointment, it is necessary not just for you to survive, but for you to thrive.

Exercise: ABC Problem-Solving

When it comes to conflict, it's hard to know where to start in terms of finding a productive and valuable solution. One method to help you problem-solve is known as ABC problem-solving (Brantley et al., 2007). This stands for:

- alternatives

- best ideas

- commitment

From the moment that we sense conflict, it's easy to get tunnel vision toward one solution. Suddenly, that solution might not even be possible; therefore, we don't believe that conflict resolution is possible at all. When ABC problem-solving, start with alternatives. There is always more than one option, even when you can only think of the first. Ask for advice. Seek past experiences to help you come up with a third, fourth, or fifth option.

Next, move on to the best ideas out of all of the alternatives that you came up with. Pick the top ones that seem the most logical and possible. Think of all possible outcomes when assessing which is best.

Finally, that takes us to commitment. Once you come up with the best idea and you determine what steps to take next, you then have to actually commit to that. This is an important part of ABC problem-solving, because we have to commit ourselves to learning from our mistakes. Having to pick the alternative, third, or fourth option doesn't always feel great. You had your mindset on the first option. You had a backup plan, and even that fell through. Now you're going with the last option, so it's easy to let things fizzle out and want to avoid the situation altogether. However, making a commitment means that you are dedicating yourself to at least following through, so even if things do end up in the worst-case scenario, you have a learning experience.

Acceptance

Accepting the moment for what it is and stopping trying to change it will make times of crisis easier to work through. Suffering arises when we fail to accept reality, creating resistance (Vaughn, n.d.-b). Stopping the resistance means allowing your body to find peace with the moment, lessening the side effects of intense emotions.

Examples of scenarios when you might use acceptance skills:

- Your partner breaks up with you, even though you'd still want to work out the relationship.

- You didn't get the job you were planning on getting.

- You fell into an old self-harm pattern and now feel regretful for the choices you made.

- You lashed out and had a heated, emotional fight with your best friend, and now they won't talk to you.

There are many situations that we can't change. The most we can do is learn from the situation and then accept the moment.

Exercise: Missing-Links Analysis

Flow charts are very helpful when trying to identify various emotions. They can also be used to help determine what was missing from an interaction that could have actually helped to prevent conflict. The missing-link analysis method is an exercise to use to figure out why unwanted emotions led to ineffective behavior (Lineham, 2015).

By following a certain chain of investigation, you can determine what the missing link was, therefore preventing it from happening again. What got in the way of effective behavior? This can be answered in a few steps:

1. First, identify the best possible solution. Do you know what was the best thing to do before the situation happened? Did you have an idea of the most ideal behavior? If you didn't, then you couldn't have done much, and now it's important to take this behavior as a learning experience to ensure that behavioral effects are reduced in the future. If you did know, you can then move on to the next part of the flowchart.

2. What was it that depleted motivation? Even though you knew what the right thing to do was, you still chose not to, so now you must find what it was that stopped you from making that choice. Was it a lack of energy? A lack of important resources? Is there something that got in the way of delaying your reaction? If yes, then you can identify what this was and ensure that it doesn't arise again in the future. If there wasn't a lack of motivation, it's then important to evaluate what was blocking your reasonable thinking.

3. Are there triggering or impulsive sources that block reasonable thinking? Did past feelings arise that made you want to act in a certain way? Did you operate under the belief that something else would be the outcome? After finding the preferred behavior, motivational block, and distracting thought, you will then be able to find the missing link, therefore preventing this behavior in the future.

This involves a little more investigation. Sometimes you might believe that you failed to do homework because you simply did not feel like doing homework. Dive deeper. Something else was blocking you, and when you find that missing link, it will all click and make more sense. Create a chain of your behavior to find what missing link was needed to bring it all together.

Exercise: Radical Acceptance

In a world where it's easy to turn our heads to the things that we don't like and deny everything we don't agree with, actually accepting our situation feels radical.

There will always be other people to validate the negative emotions that you feel. Any belief system that you hold can be shared with somebody else in the world. This means that we can live in a place of resistance. You can get stuck in a cycle of following things that you know aren't good for you, and that can lead to more chaotic or potentially harmful emotions. Radical acceptance means embracing the events around you as reality rather than finding justification or having to come up with a logical solution to everything you feel (*Radical Acceptance*, n.d.). You can radically accept what has happened. You could embrace this as being a necessary or needed situation that you are enduring. This might involve believing that there is something down the line that will make everything make sense. Even when you feel like you exist in a terrible moment, radical acceptance means sitting with those feelings and not necessarily needing a solution.

The opposite of radical acceptance is resistance. Resistance means casting blame. It's easy to go back through every little point in your life and blame small pieces for the reason why you ended up where you are today. If you're struggling with money, you might think back to that extravagant purchase you made three years ago. What if you had just saved that money instead? If a friend hurts you, you might think back to a time a few months ago when you should have cut them off to prevent yourself from getting hurt once again. The reality is, we can't go back in time. Trying to cast blame on all these little moments in the past is your way of existing in resistance and denial.

You don't have to have a solution, a reason, or a logical explanation for every conflict that you go through. Sometimes you simply have to accept it for what it is. Only once you accept this situation as reality can you then take action. If you're constantly blaming the past for why you ended up where you are now, you fail to take any responsibility for the power that you have in this moment. You will then ignore the important steps that you should be taking to move on. Staying stuck in resistance causes you to repeat mistakes, therefore casting more blame on yourself. You'll find yourself ruminating through thoughts like, "I should have done this," or, "if only I had done that."

This creates a language in your mind where you're constantly evaluating your past behavior through a lens where you hyperfixate on small mistakes.

Radical acceptance means saying, "This happened, and now I'm going to do this." Radical acceptance means being patient and sitting with your feelings. Acceptance acknowledges that this is a fleeting feeling and that things are going to get better and move toward a more productive standpoint.

For this exercise, take a few moments to reflect on what it means to you to be resistant and to find acceptance. When were some situations where you managed to accept the moment? What are some situations where you struggled with resistance? What are some things that you still struggle to accept and that you are afraid of resisting in the future? This exercise exists mostly as a reflective activity, but feel free to journal your thoughts or share them with others to help you get a better sense of what it means to radically accept.

Empowerment

Knowing how to empower yourself through future distress gives you the strength to reduce the pain and suffering that a crisis can bring on. You will be less likely to reach a heightened state of vulnerability when you can reassure yourself that even if you do find yourself in moments of distress, you know how to get yourself out of that situation.

Examples of scenarios when you might use empowerment skills:

- You want to sign up for a class with a new skill.

- You're struggling to stick to a healthy routine.

- You want to stand up to a friend who has been putting you down.

- You recently got fired and are feeling bad about your skills, and are left wondering what to do with your life next.

Deep down, we all have strengths, powers, and abilities that contribute to the unique individuals we are. Some of us are so powerful that we end up using those skills against ourselves. Recognizing your abilities will give you the courage to face your emotions, even when they feel like too much.

Exercise: Priorities

This exercise sets out to help you assess what goals are most important to you. There are various goals you might have for your future, but knowing what to prioritize is crucial so that you can actually get these things done! Some examples of goals you might have include:

- The fulfillment of your basic needs. Are you taking care of your health? Do you struggle with the way that you physically feel? Examples of these goals might include starting an exercise routine, making dentist/doctor's appointments for checkups, or trying a plant-based diet to add more nutrition to your daily routine.

- The level of satisfaction you have with life. Are you satisfied with your career? Do you like your location? Do you want to pursue higher education? Examples of these goals might include going back to school to get a Master's degree or specific certificate, moving to a new city you've always dreamed of, or changing up your personal style.

- How do you want to influence others? Do you have dreams of becoming a motivational speaker? Maybe you want to become a well-known artist or household name in the TV world. Influential goals might include taking a writing class, starting a new social media, or studying various activists with similar goals.

- What does success mean to you? Do you want to buy a new house or reach a certain step in your career? Identify success and what that looks like in your world, and determine what goals you have pertaining to this. Examples of success goals might be to save $1,500, volunteer two hours a week, or search for a new job.

- How do you interact with those around you? Are you a friendly person that others like being around, or have you been struggling to make friends? Do you find yourself frequently fighting with loved ones, or do you perhaps find it difficult to maintain a healthy relationship? Examples of relationship goals might be to start a new online dating profile, get in touch with an estranged relative, or join a hobby class to meet like-minded individuals.

- What knowledge do you want to gain in the world? This involves different goals pertaining to your dreams in relation to your artistic abilities. Perhaps you want to explore the world and travel to discover unseen sights. Goals related to knowledge might include starting a garden, practicing painting, or going on a nature hike in a foreign country.

Fill out the chart below to help you assess what areas of life you should focus on, listed from most to least important:

Priority	Goals You Have
Basic Needs	1. 2. 3.
Satisfaction	1. 2. 3.
Influence	1. 2. 3.

Success	1.
	2.
	3.
Relationships	1.
	2.
	3.
Knowledge	1.
	2.
	3.

Now, go back through and collect all of the things you listed as being your first priority. These create different goals and objectives for you to strive for. You can use these desires as scheduled points in your future, providing a substantial goal to work toward.

Below are a few thought prompts to get your mind working if you are struggling to come up with goals. Consider these questions to get the wheels of your mind turning toward understanding your purpose, desires, and deepest hopes for the future:

- If the world ended tomorrow and you were the last person standing, how would you spend your time?

- If you won the lottery, what would you do with your time?

- If you could snap your fingers and learn any skill, what would it be?

- Which instrument, sport, or creative hobby would you want to be an expert at?

- If you could get paid to do anything, what job would you want?

- Imagine that you have a time machine and can see a glimpse into your future 20 years from now. What is one thing that would make you happy to see, and what is one thing that would make you really sad to see?

- Picture yourself sitting in the back row at your own eulogy decades from now. What do you hope others will say about you long after you are gone?

- If you were a superhero, what would your power be? What enemy would you have to fight?

- What did you want to be as a child, and does your career align with that now?

- If you had three wishes, what would you wish for?

- If you could make sure there is one thing certain about the future, what would you want that to be?

- If you could change any relationship you had, what changes would you pick, and how would that appear to the other person?

- What is the hardest thing to do, and what is the easiest?

- What is one thing that makes you feel fulfilled and satisfied?

- What is one thing that you do that you could never live without?

Exercise: Sleep Schedule

Your sleep habits are among the most powerful health-related decisions that will affect your behavior. Everything is linked to how you sleep. When sleep health is insufficient, it can cause grogginess, cognitive delay, agitation, depression, and many more serious health conditions.

When you are not well-rested, you will find that you might get into more frequent fights and conflicts with those around you. Improving sleep health isn't as simple as "getting more sleep."

Start by tracking your sleep schedule for the week. Every day, track what time you go to sleep (sleep time), and what time you wake up (waking time). Also note if you woke up frequently or tossed and turned throughout the night (full night), and whether or not you felt rested in the morning (rested).

You can use the chart below to help:

Day	Sleep Time	Waking Time	Full Night?	Rested?
Monday				
Tuesday				
Wednesday				
Thursday				
Friday				
Saturday				
Sunday				

After you have a solid idea of your current sleep health, you can then follow the tips below to troubleshoot your sleep habits and make necessary changes:

1. Aim for seven to eight hours of sleep per night. Your body goes through various chemical, hormonal, and mental stages throughout the night, and that means you need to get the proper amount for cognitive development.

2. Stay as consistent as possible with your sleep and waking times. The more consistency you have in your schedule, the easier it will be to reach that deep state of sleep.

3. Turn off all lights. Your body has signals wired within it to respond to sunlight. False lights, like from the TV, can trick your body into thinking the sun is rising, therefore triggering a more awake state. Flashing lights will also be distracting.

4. Avoid caffeine for at least six hours before you plan to go to bed, but more time is better. It's also important to delay caffeine in the morning. When you automatically start the day with strong coffee, it weakens your body's natural ability to wake itself up. Instead, start with some water and a filling meal, and then enjoy coffee later in the day when you need

an extra boost. A full glass of water is sometimes all you need to feel awake and refreshed in the morning.

5. Pick cooler temperatures to sleep with alongside minimal clothing. While you might like to be warm at night, your body naturally heats up. Use more blankets rather than more clothing or heating in order to give you a chance to alternate temperatures throughout the night.

6. Avoid long naps during the day. Keep naps short, under 30 minutes, if they are really needed.

What parts of your sleep health are lacking? It's easy to want to stay up late at night, scrolling through social media and catching up. However, when we do this, it gives us the false sense we're prolonging tomorrow's stressors when in reality, we are only adding more.

Overview: Distress Tolerance

There are five main skills to remember when increasing distress tolerance:

1. stopping

2. distraction

3. self-soothing

4. acceptance

5. empowerment

Stop emotions before they turn into something more intense. Emotions can build into something much larger when unmanaged versus letting ourselves feel them. Sometimes this means simply following distracting measures to ensure your attention is taken somewhere other than your biggest stressors. If you know how to self-soothe and care for yourself, you will build inner trust, leading to more peaceful emotions. Once you get to this state, you can learn how to accept your surroundings, therefore empowering yourself. As your emotions improve internally, you can then use those skills to help improve your personal life as well.

Chapter 5

Interpersonal Effectiveness

ONCE YOU ARE MINDFUL, managing emotions, and working through distress, you can start to focus on how to communicate your needs and wants with others. Interpersonal skills are all about how you take your emotions and manage them alongside others to prevent and manage conflict.

Many conflicts arise in relationships when we feel as though our needs are not being met. This can cause conflicts and heightened fights, whether it's a romantic or strictly professional relationship.

Beyond our needs, we all have desires that can get in the way of finding a healthy resolution. When two people are clashing over wanting different things, finding a compromise and resolution can prevent further distress.

Conflict brings on heightened feelings of unwanted emotions, which could trigger even more undesirable feelings. Addressing conflict not only helps you in the moment but it will make you less fearful of conflict arising again. This, therefore, ensures you're more likely to say what you need and want, keeping an open channel of communication.

Listening is half of communication. It's important to allow others a chance to talk and to listen beyond just the words that they choose to share. This will help you get to the core of the conflict rather than existing a defensive position.

Regardless of the status of any type of relationship, emotional management is necessary to ensure that we maintain our needs and wants, and overcome conflict.

Needs

Knowing how to ask for what you need will help decrease your emotional load and increase your emotional management. This also includes knowing when you are unable to help someone else who is asking for more than what you are capable of.

Examples of scenarios when you might use needs skills:

- You're asking for a raise for the first time in ten years.

- You feel like your partner has been taking advantage of your generosity.

- A friend is pressuring you to hang out frequently and hasn't been giving you much personal space.

- Your boss just asked you to work the weekend even though they knew you were going on vacation.

Whenever it's required that we express our needs, these exercises can help.

Exercise: Assertive Vocabulary

The next important exercise to follow is the evaluation of whether or not your vocabulary has been assertive. When discussing anything with another person, whether it's a conflict or just your personal opinion, it's good to focus on "I" statements. "I" statements focus on you, your emotions, and your feelings.

Nobody else knows what you're feeling or thinking, and nobody can deny what you're feeling or thinking.

While your thoughts and feelings aren't always true or factual, the fact that you are experiencing them is something objective, and that cannot be invalidated by another person.

Alternatively, "you" statements are subjective. For example, let's say that you get into a fight with your partner. The two of you are struggling because your partner is doing some things that make it hard for you to trust them. They might not be texting you or calling you frequently throughout the day. They often hide what they do with other people, and they seem to be secretive about certain individuals that they interact with. This behavior makes you feel insecure, worried, and jealous. You worry that maybe they're having an affair or that they are simply spending time with people that you might not want them to be spending time with.

You could approach this by telling them, "You are untrustworthy," or you might say, "You are deceptive, and you are secretive."

What this does is create a defense in their mind. Now they're not focused on how you're feeling. They're not concerned with their actions and the way that they might have been influencing your emotions. Their main concern is now defending themselves. They want to prove to you that they are not untrustworthy, deceptive, or secretive. They are not going to be focused on the core of the issue at all and, instead, are going to be racking their brain for proof and evidence that they are not who you say they are.

Instead, you can focus on "I" statements in this example. You might say, "I am feeling left out. I am feeling worried about where you are. I am feeling stressed and overwhelmed when you don't keep in touch with me."

Now they have to think about how you're feeling. They are focused on your emotions, and they are less likely to feel defensive because now they're conscious about the way that they're making you feel.

Don't use this method simply to add "I" in front of "you" statements. For example, you wouldn't say, "I think you are untrustworthy."

While you did say "I," you also still made a "you" statement. Focus on what you are feeling because that is truly the only thing that cannot be argued or denied when discussing conflict with another person.

Let's think about a professional example. Lately, your boss has been cutting down your hours and now it's getting to the point where it's affecting your overall income, so you're struggling to make ends meet. You might storm into their office angry and upset. You might say:

- you are creating a toxic work environment

- you are not giving me enough hours

- you are being unfair

What your boss is going to do is then focus on their skills and qualities. They are going to get defensive and remind you that they are the boss and that they are in charge. They're going to focus on the reasons why they might not be giving you hours and defending their actions. This won't lead you to the outcome you desire.

Instead, you might walk into their office and say:

- I feel as though my hours are getting cut.

- I feel worried about my future with the company.

- I am concerned with how this is going to affect me financially.

- I am fearful of what this holds for the future of our company.

Your boss will then have to address your concerns directly rather than focusing on all the reasons that they're a good boss and that they're not being deceptive or cutting your hours. This is a hard thing to do at first. However, with practice, you will be able to get there.

Now, take some time to go through some of the feelings that you have been struggling with in terms of how others have been interacting with you. For example, if you feel as though your partner, roommate, parent, or other individual in a personal relationship has been acting a certain way, you might have a few names come to mind. How can you turn "you" statements into "I" statements?

Exercise: DEAR MAN

Sometimes managing relationships can be hard because we are focused on our own wants or needs. Resolving conflict and compromising doesn't mean that you have to give up your needs altogether! Instead, you can use the **DEAR MAN** method to help you remember the important steps of getting what you want (Lineham, 2015). This stands for:

- Describe: Explain the situation to someone else in the most objective way possible. Focus on only facts, not personal opinions or persuading points.

- Express: After stating the objective facts, you can then move on to expressing only your feelings; remember to use "I" statements and avoid accusatory remarks.

- Assert: Stay assertive with what you are sharing and be as specific as possible about any requests or criticism you are providing. The other person will not be able to guess what you want or read your mind, even if it feels like the answer is obvious to you.

- Reinforce: After presenting all of the information to the other person, you can then reiterate the benefits of what they will gain from this negotiation. Focus on what is to be gained after the fact.

- Mindful: Stay mindful of the objective points of the situation. It's easy to get lost in your emotions or to make assumptions about what the other person is thinking or feeling. However, this can lead to further issues, so practice mindfulness skills when negotiating.

- Appear: Your appearance says a lot about what you are feeling. If you show that you are worried and anxious, the other person might not trust you, even though you're simply afraid that they will say no.

- Negotiate: Know going into a negotiation that this isn't necessarily the exact way to get everything you want. There are going to be some sacrifices and compromises to make, and if you don't accept that before, it can be hard to follow the first few parts of the acronym.

Integrate this skill into your relationships whenever you want to get your point across and express your needs to others. This can help you overcome obstacles and improve relationships in the long-term.

Exercise: Modulating Intensity

It's not always what you say but how you say it. Deep inside of you lies intense emotions waiting to pour out. However, sometimes that can come off in the opposite way you intended when talking to another person. Whether you are asking for what you want or you are telling someone why they can't have what they want, it's important to modulate the intensity with which you share (*Modulating Intensity*, n.d.). There are a few ways to do this:

- Focus on the urgency of your needs. If you are feeling anxious and overwhelmed, you might come off angry and fearful to another person. They will feed off of this energy rather than helping you have your needs met. Identify what need is being met and how quickly you need help with reaching your goals.

- Identify the consequence of not getting needs. This can be shared with the other person when reiterating what need you must have filled. This is also an important aspect to focus on when someone else is asking for their needs to be met, but you're not able to do so.

- Consider the vulnerability of their ability to help. Are you asking a lot of them, or are you asking a favor that they've fulfilled before? Are you asking them something you know is going to make them upset? When you evaluate this, it will be easier to manage your tone.

- What is expected or asked of them? How might you inconvenience them when turning down their offer or making a large request?

- Consider situational aspects. For example, asking your boss for help right before lunch might make you less likely to get what you want, versus asking them toward the end of the day when they are in a good mood and ready to head home.

- Make sure to give time to others 'decisions. When we use too high of a level of intensity when making requests, it can add pressure, and many will crack under that pressure!

The intensity of your decisions is based on what's going on around you. Be mindful of the situation when determining how to ask for something you want or need or how to best say "no."

Wants

Beyond our basic needs, we also deserve things we want. Going forward, it's crucial to know how to set boundaries with others to protect and gain the things you want.

Examples of scenarios when you might use want skills:

- You feel like your partner has been disregarding your personal goals and professional dreams.

- You've been feeling prioritized last and are burnt out from taking care of others.

- You feel lost and as if you don't have a purpose or sense of direction.

Though we have endless thoughts all day long, we can sometimes get to a point where we don't know who we truly are. Disconnecting from yourself in this type of way can make it hard to stay ahead of influential emotions. Redefining your wants and value system is a good place to start as you rebuild your relationship with yourself.

Exercise: Your Wants

We can be so driven by emotions and influences in life that we lose sight of the things we need and what other aspects we actually want. Fill out the chart below based on the following headings:

1. Your needs: These are the basic necessities required for survival.

2. Your rights: These are the basic human things you deserve, alongside other boundaries.

3. Things you enjoy: These are the things that actually bring you joy.

The important distinction to make here is that your wants are different from your needs. Having your needs met should be standard. These are our rights—the things we all deserve. By categorizing these into different columns, you will be able to decipher what you actually deserve versus what wants you have been neglecting. Some examples have been added to the chart:

Needs	Rights	Enjoyment
food water shelter validation love / family socialization	Respect Bodily autonomy Accessibility Fill in your personal boundaries below:	These are personal things to you that you find enjoyment from:

Add any other needs that you feel weren't covered:		

At first, it can be hard to tell the difference between what you need, what you have a right to, and what you enjoy. Once you know the difference, you can then facilitate self-care to ensure your needs are met. After this, you can then ensure your lifestyle and the people around you not only allow but help assist in getting the things you want.

Exercise: Value System

One way to assess your wants for the future is to try the valued living questionnaire developed by Kelly Wilson (Wilson et al., 2002). This has responders assess ten areas:

1. family

2. romantic/intimate relationships

3. parenting

4. social life

5. work

6. education

7. recreation

8. spirituality

9. community

10. self-care

Looking back on these 10 aspects, go through and rate them on a scale of 1-10. You should come up with two ratings based on:

- how important you feel these aspects are

- how you believe you are fulfilling these aspects

Afterwards, you can then compare these values. For example, if you rate family as being a level 10 importance, but a level one based on how you are fulfilling familial roles, that might indicate that this is a place for improvement. You might rate self-care as being a level "10" importance but you gave it a "two" in terms of how well you have been caring for yourself.

This value system helps to align your actions with your beliefs. When we are not following a strong value system, it can make us feel as though we are failing to dedicate important attention to the things we desire the most.

Conflict

Conflict is inevitable, whether it is with ourselves or those around us. Existing in a place where you are afraid of conflict can keep you from speaking up or asking for what you want. Rather than trying hard to prevent the inevitable, changing your attitude can help. Prepare for, and stay calm through conflict for proper relationship management.

Examples of scenarios when you might use conflict skills:

- You and a coworker don't see eye to eye on a work issue.

- Your ex-partner is getting argumentative about who will have custody this upcoming holiday.

- Your sibling and a parent keep putting you in the middle of their fights.

Conflict can be scary because it gives us a sense that the relationship is at risk. In reality, conflict is a way to repair and mend our relationships, allowing us to get more from them in the end.

Exercise: GIVE

Relationships are complicated at times, but even when the going gets rough, you can find ways to help you and the other person work through these various conflicts. An acronym to help you remember how to maintain relationships is the GIVE acronym (Lineham, 2015). This stands for:

- Gentle: Use a gentle tone when talking with others. No matter how intense the conflict is, you can always talk in a soothing or low voice so as to not add agitation to their already heightened state. This also ensures you stay physically gentle to avoid fighting, hitting, or hurting others in any way.

- Interested: Show that you are interested in what they have to say or share. Even though you might be upset with them, or you are struggling to see where they are coming from, you can at least show that you are attempting to hear what they have to say.

- Validate: Validation does not have to be confused with approval. They can feel the way they feel while you also feel the way you feel. Validation shows that you understand they are humans with emotions. After you acknowledge the way they feel, you will find that it's much easier to work through conflict.

- Easy manner: Keep an easy manner when talking to others. Use humor or other light-hearted responses to keep the tone from getting too intense. Having an easy manner ensures that you don't contribute to aggressive behavior.

Relationships are all about give and take. Do your part to make contributions and sacrifices to the relationship, and most importantly, GIVE.

Exercise: Barriers

There are three main barriers keeping you from effective communication as it stands (*Barriers to Interpersonal Effectiveness*, n.d.):

- Existing barriers: These are developed habits over time, such as aggression patterns. What you learned in childhood and what you learned as an adult can impact how you interact with others.

- Needs Threats: Whether you feel as though something is lacking in your life or you are afraid of losing something you already have, any sort of loss or insult to our needs can create communication barriers.

- Perspective: How you view the world will change how you interact with the world. Heightened fear patterns, such as expecting the worst, can make it hard to express what you want. This might also include past experiences endured.

Once you break down the barriers that are causing communication conflict, it will be much easier to come up with effective ways of jumping over barriers. How can you build bridges, ladders, and stairs to surpass the boundaries restricting you? First, know what they are, and then you can use some of the other skills learned in the book to overcome them.

Listening

A huge part of a healthy relationship is knowing how to communicate, and half of communication is listening. It can be hard to work through conflict if you're focused on what to say next rather than really listening to the other person to work through issues. Listening helps you see the pathway to get to a place of mutual satisfaction, not just one where one party benefits more than the other.

Examples of scenarios when you might use listening skills:

- Your partner wants to open up about something they've been struggling with.

- Your child is having a tantrum and getting frustrated.

- Your boss is clarifying recent changes that, at first, caused your team to panic.

Listening happens through verbal tone, body language, and the background situation. What someone actually says is important, but there are many hidden messages behind what others are sharing. When we really open up and allow them to share, we can see a bigger picture that helps get to the root of many issues.

Exercise: Give Attention

No matter what conversation you're having with another person, giving them attention is necessary to ensure that their needs are also being met. If you and the other person are struggling with a large conflict, it might be hard to give them attention. You might be feeling frustrated with what they're saying, and you would prefer to give your attention elsewhere. You might be focused on your feelings and your own emotions and running through all of the things that you want to say to them in your head. The next exercise involves giving attention to others.

Whatever conversation you have, really focus on their perspective. Ask them what they are feeling. What is wrong with the situation? What do they need to tell you? What form of communication must be shared between the two of you? Consider how they are feeling. What events leading up to this conversation, have they been dealing with? What things in the past have they been struggling with that you want to check in with them now? When can you go back to a past experience that they shared with you? Recalling a past emotion that they shared with you will show them that you remember what they were talking about. It shows you are concerned about their struggle, and this can make them feel more connected to you.

When you have a stronger connection with the other person, they'll have a greater willingness to work with you and find resolve from the situation. When you are talking to another person and giving them your attention, it's important to always ask them how they think or feel rather than telling them.

As you're working through the different skills and building your own emotional intelligence, you can then use this to connect with others and help them make better sense of what they are experiencing. Be mindful about what they're sharing with you, and notice the small ways that they are trying to express messages beyond just the words that they're saying.

Exercise: Validation

There are many social conversations that center around other people looking for validation for the things that they already know. They don't necessarily need advice or new solutions from you. Many people have their minds made up, and they are seeking validation to feel better.

As a friend or partner, you are somebody who can provide validation to the other person. By giving this to them, they will feel a sense of security around you, therefore strengthening your relationship. When validating, there are a few important steps to follow up.

1. Restate their pain point. Say it word for word, and don't try to change what they said or add a new meaning to what was shared.

2. For example, if somebody says, "I've been really struggling with work lately, and I can't seem to get anything done," don't say that they have been feeling stressed or overwhelmed. This can then cause them to focus on arguing with your point, rather than actually feeling understood. Say what they told you objectively.

3. Make sure to use a neutral tone and don't add judgment or criticism when evaluating what they told you. Don't overgeneralize or add additional facts to their statement because this can confuse them when they might already be struggling with their emotions.

4. Use your words as a guide to get them to open up and share more. Give them compliments, especially if you are going to be offering any feedback. For example, you can remind them that they are strong or that they are resilient. You can tell them that you admire their strength and their ability to get through this situation.

5. Encourage them and let them know that what they are feeling is normal and expected. Remind them of their rights if they are struggling. If they are showing signs of guilt or they are feeling overwhelmed, remind them that they have the right to be tired. They have the right to get their basic needs met.

6. Offer to help with their needs, or ask them if there's anything that you can do. Try to be specific with this.

Validation is a great pathway to creating a system of open and honest communication. Sometimes it's hard to give validation because we don't want to invalidate ourselves in the process. However, it's crucial to remember that both individuals can feel just and valid in their emotions; not every situation only allows for one or the other to be "right."

Exercise: Mindfulness of Others

Mindfulness isn't something that we just do for ourselves. It's not a way for only you to understand your own thoughts, feelings, and emotions. Mindfulness is also a way that we can make a better sense of what the people around us are also experiencing. By doing this, you increase your empathic abilities. This can help tremendously with resolving conflict. You can also gain more meaning from what others are saying when you apply all of the extenuating circumstances to the evaluation of your interactions.

There are a few important steps to follow when you are being mindful of others.

1. The first step is to observe. Simply focus on the moment, identify the colors around you, and be present on what they are specifically saying. Pay attention to the words that are coming out of others 'mouths.

2. Visualize the words in your own mind as you are listening to help keep you focused on the things that they are sharing.

3. Pay attention to what they're wearing, how their hair is arranged, and any other observational characteristics that are related to the situation at hand.

4. Identify what senses they are experiencing. What are they seeing, smelling, hearing, touching, or tasting? These factors can greatly change how someone interacts in a situation. By evaluating their five senses, you will then be able to evaluate how this might be affecting their mood.

5. The next thing to do when being mindful of others is to withhold judgment. When you are being mindful in the moment, it's important for you not to state that a situation is "bad" or "good." It's important to apply the same rules when evaluating and being mindful of the other person. Stay neutral and withhold any judgment or strong reactions as they're sharing things with you. Lastly, it's important to fully participate. Engage with them and ask questions when you are not sure what to say. It is good to default to the "who," "what," "where," "when," or "why" of the things that they are sharing with you.

Practicing mindfulness is something you can do on your own and with others. If you notice someone is feeling anxious, you can also try to draw their focus objectively to the situation. For example, you might point out an art piece on the wall or the weather based on what the sky looks like. This can help draw a person's attention away momentarily, giving everyone a sense of mindfulness in the present moment.

Relationships

Relationships refer to any connection we have with someone else. Some relationships are very influential in our lives, like having a partner or family. Other relationships might not feel as significant, like with a coworker or the barista who brings you coffee every morning. Regardless of the intensity of the relationship, all of them need to be managed for our mental health. The remaining of these skills can be beneficial in any type of the example scenarios discussed previously.

Exercise: RAVEN Negotiating

There will be many situations in the future when you might need to negotiate. The RAVEN acronym can help (Brantley et al., 2007). This stands for:

1. Relax: Keep a calm and collected demeanor. Showing stress through tense shoulders, angry facial expressions, or furrowed brows will make the other person more anxious before negotiations have a chance to start.

2. Avoid: Avoid unwanted emotions and worsening issues that might inflate conflict. Stop conflict where it is and start the process of reducing your feelings.

3. Validate: Remember, this is not to be confused with agreement. Restate their standpoint back to them to show that you are listening and that you have an understanding of where they're coming from. This will alleviate initial tension, opening up the door to healthier communication.

4. Examine: What is the value of the conflict, and what is the motivation behind what is going on? When you can identify these two factors, you enable yourself to find the core and root issues, providing a better chance of finding specific resolutions.

5. Neutral: No matter what, maintain a neutral composure to assist in the resolution process. Showing defensiveness and offensiveness can creep into how you talk, therefore inspiring similar emotions in the other person.

Conflict is stressful, difficult, and something many of us would like to avoid. Unfortunately, for many, it is inevitable, so using techniques like **RAVEN** negotiating can give you the empowerment needed to know that you will make it through the conflict.

Exercise: THINK

Going forward, no matter what happens within your personal, romantic, and even professional relationships, the THINK acronym is a great one to remember. This ensures that you stay mindful in the moment and focused on finding productive resolution rather than heightening the conflict already present. This stands for (*DBT Interpersonal Effectiveness*, n.d.):

- T: think

- H: have empathy

- I: interpretations

- N: notice

- K: kindness

Start by thinking of what aspects you might not be aware of. There are many different perspectives that the other person might hold, all of which influence the way they behave. Think about their past, present, and future.

Have empathy. You never know what they are going through. They might be showing aggression, but perhaps something else is going on in their life. At the very least, empathy can help you find a solution if they are struggling to have their needs met.

Remember that we all have our own interpretation of what happens in life. This is based on perspective, fears, wants, desires, and everything else that makes us the unique people we are. How might the other person be making interpretations? Consider this in order to improve relationships.

Notice the mindful aspects of the situation. Recall any one of the mindfulness skills learned in this book to help you get the full picture.

At the end of the day, kindness will be a powerful tool when dealing with conflict. When they call you a name, be kind. When they push your buttons, show kindness. When they are being aggressive, use a kind tone. While it might be hard, practicing the activities discussed throughout the book can assist in the learning process.

Overview: Interpersonal Effectiveness

There are five main skills to remember when enhancing interpersonal effectiveness:

1. identify needs

2. identify wants

3. conflict resolution

4. listening

5. relationship improvement

Knowing what you need and what you want involves two different steps. Both are just as important as the other to ensure that you stay on track in getting the things that you want to live a happy and thriving life. This will also strengthen your ability to find conflict resolution and work through your biggest relationship issues. Remember the importance of listening. What others share with you extends beyond just the words that leave their mouth. Overall, relationship improvement will make your life much better. You can avoid conflict, get the things you want, and find deeper and more meaningful connections with the people who mean the most to you.

Conclusion

GOING FORWARD, the most important thing to remember about dialectical behavior skills is to make practice consistent. Try an exercise and then reflect afterward. Challenge yourself to do one or two exercises a day. Repeat them over a period of a few consecutive days if you find that you are struggling with a specific concept. Sometimes it might take a try or two to fully understand the complexities of your emotions.

Keep in mind that you also won't reach a state where you fully know everything there is to know about your emotions. Time and perspective shape your feelings into formations you couldn't have previously predicted. Keep an open mindset when emotionally exploring, and don't assume you have it all figured out.

Internally, you have a relationship with yourself to nourish. Use interpersonal skills to help you work through conflicting emotions. Seek mindfulness and coping skills to keep you emotionally regulated. Together, the core foundations of DBT will provide you with all the steps needed to reduce emotional dysregulation. Once you're able to be more mindful in the moment, you will also notice your relationships improving. Perhaps the most life-saving will be the reduction of self-destructive behavior.

Remember the four core parts of DBT:

- mindfulness

- emotional regulation

- distress tolerance

- interpersonal effectiveness

Exercises will be more effective when practiced more than once. After completing them the first time, use a journal to help track your progress. Mark down dates so you can go back and look at how you've managed to change.

DBT is powerful and can change your mindset. There might be times when you struggle with regression. Perhaps one day, you are triggered and have the worst fight yet. Perhaps you feel more depressed than you ever have before. The important thing to remember is that you will get through everything that comes your way. No matter how intense emotions feel, they will subside. Your biggest challenges will be temporary, fleeting, and some will even become learning experiences. The thoughts and feelings you endure are part of the human experience. What you have lived through and what you will live through in the future all play vital roles in creating the person you are as you exist now. Don't fight them; work with them to figure out what your body is trying to tell you through your mind's expression.

References

Amstadter, A. (2008). *Emotion regulation and anxiety disorders.* NIH.
   https://www.ncbi.nlm.nih.gov/pmc/articles/PMC2736046/

Anxiety disorders - facts & statistics. (n.d.). ADAA. https://adaa.org/understanding-anxiety/facts-
   statistics

Barriers to interpersonal effectiveness. (n.d.). DBT.
   https://dialecticalbehaviortherapy.com/interpersonal-effectiveness/barriers-to-interpersonal-
   effectiveness/

Brantley, J., McKay, M., & Wood, J. (2007). The dialectical behavior therapy skills workbook. New
   Harbinger Publications

Bray, S. (2013, February 15). *Core mindfulness in dialectical behavior therapy.* Good Therapy.
   https://www.goodtherapy.org/blog/core-mindfulness-dialectical-behavior-therapy-0215134

Chapman, A. (2006, September 3). *Dialectical behavior therapy.* NIH.
   https://www.ncbi.nlm.nih.gov/pmc/articles/PMC2963469/

DBT interpersonal effectiveness skills: the guide to healthy relationships. (n.d.). Sunrise.
   https://sunrisertc.com/interpersonal-effectiveness/

Emotion. (n.d.). Merriam-Webster. https://www.merriam-webster.com/dictionary/emotions

Emotional regulation skills. (n.d.). DBT Tools. https://dbt.tools/emotional_regulation/index.php

Groom, J., & Wilson, K. G. (2002). *The valued living questionnaire.* PDF. https://div12.org/wp-content/uploads/2015/06/Valued-Living-Questionnaire.pdf

Guenther, K. (2022). *DBT mindfulness skill: participate.* DBT Center of Orange County. https://www.dbtcenteroc.com/dbt-mindfulness-skill-participate/

Lineham, M. (2015). *DBT skills training handouts and worksheets.* (Second Edition.) The Guilford Press.

MacCann, C. (2021, January 15). *What are emotions?* Psychology Today. https://www.psychologytoday.com/us/blog/dealing-emotions/202101/what-are-emotions

Modulating intensity. (n.d.). DBT. https://dialecticalbehaviortherapy.com/interpersonal-effectiveness/modulating-intensity/

Opposite action skill. (n.d.). DBT. https://dbt.tools/emotional_regulation/opposite-action.php

Pierce, L. (2021, January 22). *Dialectical behavior therapy for OCD.* Verywell Mind. https://www.verywellmind.com/ocd-dbt-skills-2510652

Radical acceptance. (n.d.). DBT. https://dialecticalbehaviortherapy.com/distress-tolerance/radical-acceptance/

Responding rather than reaction. (n.d.). Westside DBT. https://westsidedbt.com/responding-rather-than-reacting/

Rosenthal, J. (n.d.). *Dialectical behavior therapy (DBT) distress tolerance skills: TIPP skills.* MPG. https://manhattanpsychologygroup.com/dbt-tipp-skills/

Survive a crisis situation with DBT distress tolerance skills. (2019, August 26). Skyland Trail. https://www.skylandtrail.org/survive-a-crisis-situation-with-dbt-distress-tolerance-skills/

Vaughn, S. (n.d.a). *DBT emotion regulation skills: emotion psychoeducation and mindfulness.* Psychotherapy Academy. https://psychotherapyacademy.org/section/emotion-regulation-module/

Vaughn, S. (n.d.b) *DBT distress tolerance skills: tip skill, stop skill, and more.* Psychotherapy Academy. https://psychotherapyacademy.org/section/distress-tolerance-skills/

What is cognitive behavioral therapy? (2017). Posttraumatic Stress Disorder. https://www.apa.org/ptsd-guideline/patients-and-families/cognitive-behavioral

Made in the USA
Las Vegas, NV
22 November 2023

81336491R00085